GHAZWAS AND SARIYAS

GHAZWAS AND SARIYAS

EDWARD SELL

GYAN

Published by

Gyan Publishing House
5, Ansari Road
Daryaganj, New Delhi-110002
Phone: 011-47034999, 9811692060
E-mail: books@gyanbooks.com

Distribution Network
gyanbooks.com
India, USA, Canada, UK, Australia

ISBN: 978-93-7414-289-9 (PB)

First Published, 1911

2nd Impression 2026

Printed at: Gyan Press, Delhi.

GHAZWAS AND SARIYAS
Author: EDWARD SELL

The Islam Series

GENERAL EDITOR

The Rev. Canon Sell, D.D., M.R.A.S.

GHAZWAS AND SARIYAS

GHAZWAS AND SARIYAS

BY

THE REV. CANON SELL, D.D., M.R.A.S.

FELLOW OF THE UNIVERSITY OF MADRAS

AUTHOR OF 'THE FAITH OF ISLÁM', 'THE RELIGIOUS ORDERS OF ISLÁM', 'THE HISTORICAL DEVELOPMENT OF THE QUR'ÁN', 'THE CULT OF 'ALÍ', 'THE DRUSES', 'ISLÁM: ITS RISE AND PROGRESS'

THE CHRISTIAN LITERATURE SOCIETY FOR INDIA

LONDON, MADRAS AND COLOMBO

1911

PREFACE

Two of the most important battles, Badr and Uḥud, are not described in this book. A description of them is given in another book of this series, known as *The Battles of Badr and Uḥud.* The two books taken together give a complete account of the conflicts of importance. I have only omitted Sariyas which were not of much consequence, and the results of which seem to me to have had no effect upon the history of the time or on the career of Muḥammad. I have tried to understand the modern apologies for some of these conflicts and to show why I consider them ineffective.

E. S.

January 1, 1911.

CONTENTS

	Page
SARIYAS OF HAMZA, 'UBAIDA, AND SA'D ...	3
GHAZWA OF ABWA	5
GHAZWAS OF BUWAT AND 'USHAIRA	6
SARIYA OF NAKHLA	7
GHAZWA OF THE BANI QAINUQA'	16
SARIYA OF ABU SALMA	18
SARIYA OF 'ABDU'LLAH BIN UNAIS	19
SARIYA OF BIR MA'UNA	21
GHAZWA OF THE BANI NADIR	24
GHAZWA OF THE LESSER BADR	33
GHAZWA OF THE BANI MUSTALIQ	36
GHAZWA OF THE DITCH	39
GHAZWA OF THE BANI QURAIZA	44
SARIYA OF ZAID BIN HARITHA	57
SARIYA OF 'ARNIYYA	57
GHAZWA OF HUDAIBIYA	58
GHAZWA OF KHAIBAR	60
SARIYA OF MUTA	66
CAPTURE OF MECCA	69
GHAZWA OF HUNAIN	74
GHAZWA OF TA'IF	76
GHAZWA OF TABUK	78
SARIYA OF USAMA	84

GHAZWAS AND SARIYAS

MUḤAMMAD and his Companions, soon after their arrival at Madína, began to feel the effects of poverty. The Muslim authorities[1] give full details and describe how some of the Muhájirún (the immigrants), the men who came to Madína with Muḥammad, had no homes, but slept in the mosque or a sheltered pavement outside and were known as 'Men of the pavement'. The Anṣár (helpers), the men of Madína, who invited the Prophet to come to their city, gave some employment to the immigrants, but they could only do unskilled work. 'Alí is said to have earned a few dates by carrying buckets of water. They were more successful as petty shopkeepers. Abú Bakr sold clothes; 'Uthmán retailed dates; 'Abdu'r-Raḥmán provided milk. The Prophet shared the poverty of the Muslims, and according to Tirmidhi, his face was often pinched with hunger. Alms were given to him, but these he shared with the rest. 'Áyesha states that, for considerable periods of time, they had no fires with which to cook their

[1] These are cited by Margoliouth in *Mohammed*, pp. 234-7.

food and lived on dates and water. At her wedding, seven months after the Prophet's arrival in Madína, there was no feast. 'Alí at one time made preparations for carrying on foreign trade, but his plans came to nothing, and as Muḥammad could ill spare him from Madína, a second venture was not made. 'Alí then married Fáṭima, stayed at home, and gave up all thoughts of becoming a travelling merchant. He was poor and Fáṭima complained about her lack of means. At first, she objected to the marriage on account of 'Alí's poverty, and Muḥammad asked 'Alí what he possessed. He said that he had a horse and armour. Muḥammad said: 'the horse you need, sell the armour'. He did so and the money realized 480 dirhems which were given to Billál and Amm Salíma for the wedding expenses.[1] Money might have been raised by taxation, but it would have been an unwelcome proceeding. The Jews, intelligent and industrious, were comparatively wealthy; but they were not disposed to give money to support the immigrants. They required interest and security on their loans, and so treasured up against themselves the future ill-will of the Muslims.

Thus a few months' residence in Madína brought home to the mind of the Prophet the distressed condition of his people and the helpless prospect

[1] *Muddáriju'n-Nabúwat*, p. 552.

which lay before them. The constant tribal feuds in Arabia would seem to have raised the act of capturing caravans of merchandize above that of mere robbery. It became the natural result of a dispute. This is the most charitable construction to put on the forthcoming action of the Prophet. The Meccans sent forth trading caravans. Muḥammad needed property badly. Here was a very good way of obtaining it. This is, at least, a possible reason for the commencement of the earlier raids made under the Prophet's orders. Later on, when the Meccans became alive to the danger their commerce was in, and took active measures to protect it, the wars were sometimes of a defensive nature. There were many expeditions. One commanded by the Prophet in person was called a Ghazwa. One placed in charge of one of his lieutenants is known as a Sariya. The numbers of each vary. The Ghazwas are said by some authorities to have been nineteen or twenty-four or twenty-seven, but the lower numbers omit the battles of Badr and of Uḥud, some of the attacks on the Jews, the raid on Khaibar and the conquest of Mecca. The Sariyas are very numerous.

THE SARIYAS OF HAMZA, 'UBAIDA, AND SA'D

On the seventh day of the month Ramaḍán, that is seven months after his arrival in Madína,

Muḥammad appointed Ḥamza bin 'Abdu'l-Muṭṭalib to the charge of a small expedition, and presented him with a banner. The reason for this expedition is said to have been as follows: 'When it came to the august hearing of his Lordship that a number of the Quraish were just returning from a commercial journey from Syria to Mecca, he prepared a banner and ordered Ḥamza to hasten with thirty Muhájirún to attack the caravan'.[1] This expedition was unsuccessful.

The next month another Sariya was commanded by 'Ubaida binu'l-Ḥáritha, and had for its object the capture of a caravan belonging to merchants of Mecca, under the leadership of Abú Sufyán. On this occasion some arrows were shot. Sa'd bin Abi'l-Waqqáṣ is famed as 'he who shot the first arrow for Islám'. Whether the heart of the leader failed him when he saw the greater number of the Meccans, or whether they, treating the Muslims with contempt, went their way is not clear, but nothing came of this raid.

The next Sariya was also commanded by Sa'd bin Abi'l-Waqqáṣ and started two months later in pursuit of a caravan, but the expedition arrived too late and again no booty was gained.

To give some religious sanction to these undertakings, it was now that the verse of slaughter was revealed:—

[1] *Rauḍatu's-Ṣafá*, part II, vol. i, p. 275.

> When ye encounter the infidels strike off their heads till ye have made a great slaughter among them and of the rest make fast the fetters.—Súratu Muhammad (xlvii) 4.[1]

GHAZWA OF ABWA

The early expeditions of his lieutenants having failed to secure the property so much needed, Muḥammad proceeded to lead some in person. The first of these took place in June 623. It is known as the Ghazwa of Abwá, and was as usual in pursuit of a Quraish caravan[2] which was again missed. Its chief interest, however, lies in the fact that Muḥammad made a treaty with the Bani Dhamra, a branch of the Quraish, and then returned to Madína. This was the first treaty made with a pagan tribe. Obviously, if the Meccan caravans were the object of all these raids, it was a politic act to secure, at least, the neutrality of the tribes through whose territory such caravans would pass. The idea of a treaty with the richer Meccan merchants was not sought for at this time of distress. The justification for this difference of procedure is found in a revelation:—

> God doth not forbid you to deal with kindness and fairness toward those who have not made war upon you on account of your religion, or driven you forth from your homes: for God loveth those who act with fairness.

[1] This verse refers to the Meccans and other Arab idolaters.

[2] *Mudáriju'n-Nabúwat*, p. 554.

Only doth God forbid you to make friends of those who, on account of your religion, have warred against you and have driven you forth from your homes and have aided those who drove you forth: and whoever maketh friends of them are wrong-doers.—Súratu'l-Mumtaḥina (lx) 8–9.

THE GHAZWAS OF BUWAT AND 'USHAIRA

A month later the next Ghazwa, that of Buwáṭ, was made. Buwáṭ was situated on the caravan route and so was a suitable place for a raid on passing merchants. The historians say that the raid was for the purpose of capturing a Quraish caravan. Muḥammad left Madína in charge of two trusty lieutenants, taking with him two hundred men. Some of these were citizens of Madína, a fact which shows that the Prophet's influence was now increasing in the city. Again he had to return empty-handed, for the caravan eluded his pursuit.

After a few months Muḥammad set out on a third Ghazwa, that of 'Ushaira. He set forth with 150 men, or as some say with 200 followers. This time it was to waylay a caravan rich with goods under the command of Abú Sufyán, which was on its way to Syria. Again, as regards the capture of the caravan he was unsuccessful, for it had already passed 'Ushaira, but the expedition was not in vain, for he concluded a treaty with the Bani Mudlíj. In this way he was gradually persuading a number of Arab pagan tribes to remain neutral. The historians relate how on this occasion 'Alí got the sobriquet of Abú Turáb (father of dust). 'Umar bin Yasír and 'Alí being tired went to sleep under a date tree, growing in a sandy plain. The Prophet passed by and woke them up, and seeing 'Alí dusty addressed him thus: 'Get up O Abú Turáb.' Thus 'Alí ibn Ṭálib became known as 'Alí Abú Turáb.[1]

THE SARIYA OF NAKHLA

The next expedition is known as the Sariya of Nakhla. It was under the command of 'Abdu'-lláh ibn Jaḥsh. The preceding expeditions had failed to secure any booty. Such failure was not only inconvenient, but tended to lower the prestige of the Prophet, and to give some reason for the taunts of the Jews and unbelieving men of Madína. It was now the sacred month of Rajab, and it was a time-honoured Arab institution that in a sacred month there should be a truce between hostile tribes. Men could go about unarmed and in peace. Obviously an armed force which set this custom at defiance had a good prospect of success, and success was now sorely needed by Muḥammad and the Muslims. 'Abdu'lláh had

[1] *Mudáriju'n-Nabúwat*, p. 555; *Rauḍatu'ṣ-Ṣafá*, part II, vol. i, p. 277.

with him some twelve or, according to some authorities, eight of the leading Muhájirún, amongst whom were Sa'd bin Abí Waqqás, 'Akásha bin Muḥsin and others. The commander of the expedition was directed to proceed towards Nakhla, with sealed orders, the letter containing which was not to be opened for two days. When the letter was opened and read, it was found to contain the following order: 'Advance in the name of God the most High and Glorious and, when thou arrivest by His blessing in the valley of Nakhla with thy companions, there look out[1] for the caravan of the Quraish; because thou mayest probably derive profit therefrom. Nor must thou take any one against his will. Let those who like accompany thee and those remain who like to stay behind.'[2] The Quraish caravan, proceeding to the south from Mecca, passed through the valley of Nakhla, which was thought to be a safer route than the Syrian one. Since these raids had begun, the people in Madína knew that this route was popular among Meccan merchants and, as in a sacred month a caravan would probably be lightly guarded, the prospect of success in this Sariya would seem likely to be much greater than it had been in previous ones.

Sealed orders were given, for it was necessary

[1] مترصد is the term used in the *Mudáriju'n-Nabúwat*, p. 556.
[2] *Raudatu's-Ṣafá*, part II, vol. i, p. 278.

that the Meccans should know nothing about the purpose for which they all were setting out. When the men of the expedition heard the order read, Sa'd bin Abi Waqqáṣ and 'Utaba bin G͟hazwán conveniently lost their camels. They went in search of them and did not return. The rest proceeded on their way and, after searching diligently, found the caravan in charge of four persons. It was the first day of Rajab the sacred month, but, according to some authorities, the Muslims were doubtful whether it was that day, or the last day of the preceding month Jamádí'u'-l-Ak͟hiri; and so they did not know whether they ought to attack the caravan or not. They held a consultation and arrived at the decision 'to annihilate the caravan of aberration'.[1] Fear lest the Meccans should escape overcame their scruples.[2] The Quraish were alarmed and desired to accelerate their march, so 'Abdu'lláh bin Jaḥsh said to his friends: 'The people of the caravan are afraid. Let a man shave his head, to make them believe we are going on pilgrimage to Mecca and to free them from the apprehension.'[3] The head of 'Akásha bin Muḥsin was then shaved, which, when the Meccans saw, they said: 'The people are going on pilgrimage'. They then gave up any intention of departing, allowed their camels to roam about

1 *Rauḍatu'ṣ-Ṣafá*, part II, vol. i, p. 279.
2 See *Muddáriju'n-Nabúwat*, p. 557.
3 *Rauḍatu'ṣ-Ṣafá*, part II, vol. i, p. 279.

and began to eat their food. Seeing a good opportunity the Muslims 'made a sudden rush on the infidels, and the Muslim Wáqid bin 'Abdu'lláh killed Amr bin Khaḍramí with an arrow. 'Uthmán bin 'Abdu'lláh and Hukm bin Kisán were taken prisoners. Naufil ran away and the whole property of the caravan fell into the hands of the Muslims. This Sariya is noted as being the first in which booty was gained,[1] an adversary slain, and prisoners taken'.[2] When the Meccans received the news from Naufil it was too late to attempt to rescue the property; but they said: 'The affairs of Muḥammad will scarcely prosper, because he has disregarded a sacred month.' There is a tradition to the effect that when 'Abdu'lláh reported the whole affair to the Prophet and brought the booty, he said: 'I never commanded thee to fight in the sacred month.' But the idolaters and the Jews reproached the Muslims and said: 'Muḥammad and his followers make the unlawful lawful and shed blood and plunder in a sacred month.' The Prophet then ordered the booty to be put aside for a time and kept the two prisoners in safe custody. This offence was a serious one in the eyes of all Arabs and his followers were disconcerted about it. There seems no doubt about the fact that the raid was made in a sacred month, and whether Muḥammad

[1] *Baiḍáwí*, vol. i, p. 114. [2] Ibid., p. 279.

actually planned it so or not, he accepted the result of the wrong action of his subordinates, and proceeded to justify their part and his by a revelation:—

> They will ask thee concerning war in the Sacred Month, say: 'To war therein is bad,[1] but to turn aside from the cause of God, and to have no faith in Him and in the Sacred Temple, and to drive out its people is worse in the sight of God; and civil strife is worse than bloodshed. . . . But they who believe, and who fly their country, and fight in the cause of God may hope for God's mercy.—Súratu'l-Baqara (ii) 214-5.'

After this clear sanction to an irregular action, and this ready method of getting out of a difficulty, the booty was divided and the prisoners were ransomed. Al-Hukm, however, remained in Madína and became a Muslim. The effect of this success was great. At last the danger of want and privation seemed to be at an end. All the year round Ghazwas and Sariyas could now go on. The Meccans were to be molested at any time of the year. In future expeditions, therefore, we find the Anṣár as well as the Muhájirún taking part.

[1] We have the authority of Baiḍáwí for the connexion of this verse with the raid on Nakhla (vol. i, p. 114). He translates the 'bad' of Rodwell's translations 'To war therein is bad' as ذنب كبير 'serious sin': but goes on to say that the statement is held by most authorities to be abrogated by the verse of the sword 'Kill them wherever you shall find them' [Súratú'l-Baqara (ii) 187].

Another important consequence of this raid was that the death of Amr bin Khadram, who was under the protection of 'Utba bin Rabi'a a Quraish of some standing, led to a blood feud, which made it necessary for the Meccans to fight the Muslims of Madína. At this time the Meccans had two serious causes of complaint: the constant attempts to rob them of their goods ending in this successful one, and the treacherous slaughter of Amr bin Khadram. The Muslims were now encouraged, and soon after an attempt to seize another caravan was made, which resulted in the battle of Badr, a full account of which I have given elsewhere.[1]

With reference to these expeditions in the first and second year of Muḥammad's rule at Madína, it is only fair to state that a learned Indian Muslim, the late Maulaví Cherágh 'Alí Ṣáḥib discredits the accounts given of them.[2] He speaks of them as the '*alleged* interception' of the Quraish caravans. Of the Sariyas of Ḥamza, of 'Ubaida of Sa'd, and of the Ghazwas of Abwá, of Buwáṭ, of 'Ushaira and of Nakhla he says that the statements about them are not 'corroborated by authentic and trustworthy traditions'. The accounts are, however, given by Muslim historians of repute. At the same time, historical criticism

[1] *The Battles of Badr and of Uḥud.* (C.L.S.)

[2] Cheragh 'Alí, *Critical exposition of the Jihád*, pp. 29-31; 55-60.

may show that, as regards certain details, there may be doubt; but details, even if exaggerated, must rest on some basis of fact. The expeditions themselves are not matters of imagination. Cherágh 'Alí himself admits that the biographers ibn Isḥáq, ibn Hishám Ṭabarí, ibn Athír in the *Kámil*, and Halabi in the *Insaun'l-Aiyún* refer to the Sariya of Nakhla.

Another objection is that there is an internal improbability. It is said that the inhabitants of Madína had pledged themselves only to defend the Prophet from attack, and not to join him in any aggressive step. Therefore, it seems impossible that they should have allowed Muḥammad to take any aggressive steps against the Quraish which might involve them in great trouble. Now, it is true that there was such a compact between the Muhájirún and the Anṣár;[1] but, as a matter of fact, the Anṣár did take part in these aggressive conflicts. In the battle of Badr and thereafter they freely joined in all wars; for before that time the Prophet had given many revelations about warfare and the terms of the treaty were tacitly set aside. The Prophet was too able and too determined a man to be turned aside from any line of policy he might adopt by the opinion of a few Anṣár. That they had sufficient

1 This undertaking is to be found in the first and the second pledge of 'Aqába. See Sell's *Historical Development of the Qur'án*, pp. 83, 87, 143.

influence to restrain him from making raids is only an hypothesis. Indeed, Cherágh 'Alí only says it seemed impossible that they should allow it. It surely seems more impossible that they could prevent it, and as a matter of fact they did not. The verse about fighting in a sacred month [Súratu'l-Baqara (ii) 214] is said to refer to the Meccans fighting against the Muslims and so to discredit the fact that Muḥammad was the aggressor at Nakhla; but the verse is quoted by the historians to show that it justified an act of aggression in a sacred month. It is sought to further strengthen this excuse for a serious breach of Arab custom by saying: 'They (Meccans) will not cease to war against you.' The reference to the Meccans is there and the reason for it is plain; but the real point is—the production of a revelation to justify, what from the point of view of Arab usage and custom, was an illegal act. Baiḍáwí distinctly says the verse was revealed in connexion with 'Abdu'lláh ibn Jaḥsh, the leader of the Sariya of Nakhla. He also says that it is generally agreed that the words 'to war therein is bad' are abrogated by the verse 'kill those who join other gods with God wherever ye shall find them' [Súratu't-Tauba (ix) 5].

European historians, relying on the Muslim biographies of the Prophet, hold that the Muslims were the aggressors. Cherágh 'Alí considers that these biographies rest on weak traditions and are not, therefore, trustworthy. It is said that there 'is no proof that Muḥammad, after the Hijra, commenced hostilities against the Quraish by intercepting their caravans'. This statement can only be maintained by rejecting, not merely the incidental embellishments, but the fact of the raids stated by the biographers of the Prophet. It is said that such raids were improbable, but supporters of this theory seem entirely to forget the poverty and consequent great distress of the Muslims in the early months of their residence in Madína and how necessary it was to obtain property of some sort in some way. Thus it seems reasonable to say that it was extremely probable that raids would be made. That the Quraish had persecuted the Muslims in Mecca is true; but Madína was a long way off, and no historical evidence is given to show that for some time after the Hijra the Meccans troubled themselves much about Muḥammad and his people. At all events, those who remained behind in Mecca were not ill-treated. It was not till they found their peaceful mercantile pursuits interfered with, and their trade endangered[1] that the Meccans took to active warfare. The Quraish, indeed, showed extraordinary forbearance; but, in defence of their commercial existence, they had to take up arms and the battle of Uḥud was the result.

[1] See Muir, *The Life of Mahomet*, vol. iii, p. 77.

This battle and that of Badr are so important that I have dealt with them in a separate book to which the reader is referred.[1]

THE GHAZWA OF THE BANI QAINUQA'

Before passing on to events after the battle of Uḥud, we must notice briefly the Ghazwa against a Jewish tribe, the Bani Qainuqá'. Their ancient Arab allies, the Khazrajites, had embraced Islám in some numbers, and as the ties of the new religion were stronger than the old ones of amity and alliance, the Bani Qainuqá' were isolated and open to an easy attack, especially as the other Jewish tribes rendered them no assistance. The Prophet's attitude towards the Jews generally was now undergoing a change. About a month after the battle of Badr an opportunity arose for picking a quarrel with these Jews. The story, as given by Bukhárí and Muslim,[2] is that 'Alí wishing to marry Fáṭima and being poor intended to commence trading. He was promised help by some of the Qainuqá' merchants, but Ḥamza seeing the camels, standing ready for their loads, slew them and made a feast for his friends. 'Alí complained to Muḥammad about his loss. Muḥammad came and found his uncle Ḥamza drunk. Altogether the position was most unseemly. 'Alí's

1 *The Battles of Badr and of Uḥud.* (C.L.S.)

2 See Margoliouth's *Mohammed*, pp. 281–2.

loss was great, yet his marriage was much to be desired. The means were found in the plunder soon to be obtained.

Another story is that a Muslim woman was insulted in the bazaar of the goldsmiths, which led to a quarrel and loss of life.[1] It is also said that the Bani Qainuqá' boasted, that if they had been the Prophet's opponents at Badr, he would not have gained his victory so easily. They were also accused of having broken a treaty and so according to the *Mudáriju'n-Nabúwat*, the revelation came:—

> If thou fear treachery from any people throw back their treaty to them as thou fairly mayest for God loveth not the treacherous.—Súratu'l-Anfál (viii) 60 [2]

They refused to accept Islám, were besieged for fifteen days, defeated, expelled from their homes, and all their property was confiscated. At first it was intended to execute them all, but 'Abdu'lláh ibn Ubbai, the Khazrajite, their old ally, interceded for them; so the Prophet cursed them and the milder punishment was substituted.[3]

[1] The full account will be found in the *Mudáriju'n-Nabúwat*, p. 580 and in Muir's *Mahomet*, vol. iii, pp. 134–5.

[2] 'He ordered that their hands should be tied behind their backs, and he wished to kill them.'

حکم کرد که دستهای ایشان را بر پشت بر بندند و خواست که حکم به قتل کند .

Mudáriju'n-Nabúwat, p. 580.

[3] 'Having cursed them, he abstained from their slaughter, Ibid., p. 580.

و بر این قوم را لعنت کرده از سر خون آنها درگذشت .

'Abdu'lláh was as yet too formidable a person to be turned into an enemy: but it is to him and not to the Prophet that they owed their lives. This was the first serious attack upon the Jews, who now had no reason whatever to show any loyalty to him.

They failed to combine in these early days, and were beaten in detail. Soon the time came when no opposition on their part, even though a combined one, could be successful.

THE SARIYA OF ABU SALMA

The defeat of the battle of Uḥud lowered the prestige of Muḥammad,[1] and some of the Arab tribes took the side of the Quraish. Henceforth the Muslims were not always the aggressors, but had to defend themselves against attacks. A state of civil war had now set in. Soon after the defeat at Uḥud, Muḥammad received information that the Bani Asád intended to make a raid on Madína. Their chief Ṭulaiḥa possessed a force of horsemen and fleet camel riders, with which he hoped to be able to secure and bring away a considerable portion of the flocks of the Muslims. The Prophet wisely determined to forestall the attack and sent out Abú Salma with a hundred and fifty men, chosen from the Muhájirún and the Anṣár to

1 For the way in which he sought to counteract this, see *The Battles of Badr and Uḥud*, pp. 61-8.

stop the approach of the enemy. This is called the Sariya of Abú Salma. The Prophet instructed him thus: 'Before they know of your advance and before they collect an armed force, proceed to their territory and plunder them.' Abú Salma was successful. A large herd of camels was captured and three prisoners were taken. The plunder was divided amongst the soldiers, a share having been set apart for Muḥammad. Abú Salma, whose wound received at Uḥud, had not yet healed, suffered from the exposure on this raid and died six months later on. The Prophet married his widow Umm Salma.

THE SARIYA OF 'ABDU'LLAH BIN UNAIS

About the same time the Baní Laḥyán took up a threatening attitude. They assembled round their chief Sufyán bin Khálid at a place called 'Urna. Muḥammad then sent 'Abdu'lláh bin Unais to put Sufyán out of the way. In due course he arrived in the camp of the Baní Laḥyán and came into the presence of Sufyán who said: 'Who are you'. 'Abdu'lláh replied: 'I am of the Khuzá'i tribe. I have heard that you are preparing an army and have made preparations for the killing of Muḥammad. I wish to join you.' He was allowed to join the force. Then one night, when men were asleep, he entered the tent of Sufyán and cut off his head and, after eluding his pursuers, escaped to Madína. He laid the head at Muḥammad's feet and the historians say that the Prophet and his companions were highly elated.[1] As a token of regard Muḥammad presented him with his own staff. It is said that he used it till the day of his death and that it was buried with him.

Maulaví Cherágh 'Alí says that 'Abdu'lláh was sent only as a spy, and that no blame can be attached to Muḥammad for an act he did not order;[2] but in the *Mudáriju'n-Nabúwat* we read that he was sent for the purpose 'of killing Sufyán and to clear the plain of the religion of Islám from his wickedness and mischief'.[3] Whether this statement is correct or not, the Prophet showed his approval of the treacherous deed by the honour he bestowed upon 'Abdu'lláh.

The assassination broke up the force assembled at 'Urna and so far succeeded in its object; but it was a cowardly way of meeting enemies and it set an example which the Arabs were not slow to follow. It was a game at which two could play as Muḥammad soon found out to his cost. Retribution soon came, for Wáqidi relates[4]

1 *Rauḍatu'ṣ-Ṣafá*, part II, vol. ii, p. 414; *Mudáriju'n-Nabúwat*, p. 617.

2 *Critical Exposition of the Jihád*, p. 69.

3 عبد الله بن انیس را فرستاد تا سفیان را بقتل آرد و ساحت دین اسلام را از شر و فسادی وی پاک کرداند — p. 618.

4 *Táríkh-i-Wáqidi.* (Urdu translation, 1874), p. 267.

how, after the murder of Sufyán, the men of the Laḥyán tribe went to the 'Adhl and the Qára tribes and instigated them to request Muḥammad to send persons to instruct them in the tenets of Islám, as they wished to become Muslims. They further suggested that, when the teachers arrived, they might slay those who had killed Sufyán, and make prisoners of the rest and sell them to the Quraish. The deputation was sent and in reply to its request for teachers Muḥammad sent seven men, six of whom were natives of Madína and one, Kh̲álid bin abi'l-Bukair, was a Muhájir. In due course, they arrived at the well of Rají', where they were attacked by some armed men of the Baní Laḥyán who slew three Muslims and took three prisoners. One who tried to escape was crushed to death by pieces of rock which were hurled upon him. Thus was the assassination of Sufyán avenged.

THE SARIYA OF BIR MA'UNA

In the same month, May, A.D. 625, another serious affair happened. It is known as the Sariya of Bír Ma'úna. It is related that an aged chief of the Bani 'Ámir, named Abú Birá, paid Muḥammad a visit. He was kindly received and though he himself declined to accept Islám, he said that, if Muḥammad would send some of his followers to teach his people, there was every reason to suppose that they would become Muslims. Now the Bani 'Ámir dwelt in Najd and many of the tribes in that region were allies of the Quraish, and so Muḥammad expressed his fears for the safety of his messengers, as he had no treaty with the men of Najd. The old chief said: 'Put away all fear from your mind, they will be under my protection and I will not allow any one to molest them.' Being thus assured, Muḥammad sent seventy men, mostly men of Madína, with a few Muhájirún. The Prophet gave them a letter to the Bani 'Ámir and to the chiefs in Najd. It so happened that the old chief had resigned his leadership to his nephew 'Ámir ibn Ṭufail who was an avowed enemy of the Muslims. He put the bearer of the letter to death and, failing to get the men of his own tribe to disregard the promise of safety given to the Muslims by his uncle Abú Birá, he sought and obtained the aid of the Bani Sulaim, of which tribe members had been slain by the Muslims in the battle of Badr. They consented and 'Ámir bin Ṭufail with a considerable force went to Bír Ma'úna, where the Muslims were awaiting the return of their messenger. After a severe conflict all the Muslims were slain, with the exception of two who escaped.[1] Abú Birá, on hearing of his nephew's treachery with regard to

[1] A very full account of this affair will be found in the *Mudáriju'n-Nabúwat*, pp. 619–20.

the bearer of the letter, fell ill with grief and died. When Muḥammad heard the news of the disaster he was naturally greatly grieved, and for many days in the public prayers he called for vengeance on the treacherous assailants of his men. It is said that Gabriel brought this verse from those who were slain: 'Acquaint our people that we have met our Lord, He is well pleased with us and we are well pleased',[1] but that it was afterwards cancelled and was not included in 'Umar's rescension of the Qur'án.

This was a gross act of treachery and cannot be justified. It naturally embittered the Muslims against the pagan tribes. At the same time, it was disheartening and the supposed revelation from the men slain was intended to encourage the people generally. Muḥammad also seems to have been alarmed, for he acted with caution in the event which immediately followed. 'Amru bin Amaíya, one of the two survivors, on his way back to Madína met two men of the Bani 'Ámir. They suspected no harm and took their siesta.[2] 'Amru seized the opportunity to slay them, which was an act as treacherous as that of 'Ámir ibn Ṭufail. These men had been to see Muḥammad and were under his protection, and so the Prophet

1 بَلِغُوا عَنَّا قَوْمَنَا إِنَّا قَدْ لَقِينَا رَبَّنَا فَرَضِىَ عَنَّا وَ أَرْضَانَا

Mudáriju'n-Nabúwat, p. 620.

2 *Táríkh-i-Wáqidi*. (Urdu translation, 1874), p. 276.

was vexed at the action which 'Amru soon reported to him. Wáckidi and Tabari say that the Prophet paid, according to the custom of the Arabs, the full blood money for them to 'Ámir ibn Ṭufail and restored the property taken from them.

THE GHAZWA OF THE BANI NADIR

These sad events soon led to a very serious attack on a Jewish tribe. The Bani Naḍír were neighbours of the Bani 'Ámir, and it is said were their confederates,[1] and so Muḥammad, who was in the habit of turning to the Jews when he needed money, conceived the idea that they should now bear their share of the payment of the blood-money. Wáqidi distinctly says that he went to them for the very purpose,[2] accompanied by Muhájirún and Anṣár. The Bani Naḍír were a wealthy tribe, but one of their Rabbis, Ká'b bin Ashraf, had a short time before been assassinated,[3] and so naturally they may have thought that Muḥammad should have come to pay blood-money and not to exact it. Under the circumstances

1 Aḥláf (احلاف) which may mean confederates bound by an oath to assist them; but not necessarily liable for blood-money, for which Muir says he can find no authority; so Muḥammad had no claim on the Bani Nadír. See Muir's *Life of Mahomet*, vol. iii, p. 209.

2 *Tárikh-i-Wáqidi*, p. 276.

3 Muir, *Life of Mahomet*, vol. iii, pp. 143–4; Koëlle, *Moḥammed and Moḥammedanism*, p. 172.

the demand for help in paying blood-money might well have seemed impudent to a tribe which had a right to demand it.[1] However, they received the Prophet, who came to see them accompanied by Abú Bakr, 'Uthmán, Álí and others, courteously; but he suddenly departed and returned to Madína, giving as his reason for so doing that he had been informed by Gabriel that treachery and danger were imminent. The traditions go into some details about this, but we have only the Muslim version and not any Jewish statements about it. There is no reference in the Qur'án to any such plot, and this omission throws considerable doubt upon the story.[2] All that Súratu'l-Ḥashr (lix), the Súra which specially deals with this affair, says is to be found in the third verse which states that 'they set them against God and His apostle'. Muḥammad's followers soon joined him in Madína and this verse was then revealed:—

> O believers, recollect God's favour upon you, when certain folk were minded to stretch forth their hands upon you: but He kept their hands from you.—Súratu'l-Má'ida (v) 14.

When the Bani Naḍír found that Muḥammad had gone, they met together, and Kináya bin Ṣuwair advised them to accept Muḥammad as an apostle, for otherwise they might be ordered to emigrate

1 Margoliouth, *Mohammed*, p. 313.
2 See Muir's *Life of Mahomet*, vol. iii, pp. 301-10 and notes.

and so lose their houses and lands. The people replied that they could not give up their religion. The Prophet then sent Muḥammad bin Muslima to them. It is recorded that he charged them with treachery,[1] and said that all who did not depart within the space of ten days, would have their heads cut off.[2] They expressed their surprise that Muḥammad should send, or that a member of the Bani Aws should bring, such a message. He replied, 'Hearts are changed now' (*Wáqidi*, 280). The Jews then made preparations to obey this order, when a messenger from 'Abdu'lláh ibn Ubbai[3] arrived urging them not to go and promising assistance. It was also expected that the Bani Quraiẓa, another Jewish tribe, would come to the rescue. 'Abdu'lláh and his friend may have hoped for this aid, or for some help from Mecca, or they may have believed that the Bani Naḍír could defend their forts; but whether the advice was given in good faith or not, he failed to assist them. Whether he found it impossible to do so, or whether he intentionally broke his faith with them, is doubtful. The Qur'án accuses him and his party of insincerity:—

[1] There is no proof of this. See Muir's *Life of Mahomet*, vol. ii, p. 210 and note.

[2] Full accounts of this embassy are given by the Muslim historians. See *Táríkh-i-Wáqidi*, p. 280; *Mudáriju'n-Nabúwat*, p. 623; *Rauḍatu'ṣ-Ṣafá*, part II, vol. ii, p. 419.

[3] He was a Munáfiq, or hypocrite, a name given to those inhabitants of Madína who were not friendly to Muḥammad.

> Hast thou not observed the disaffected saying to their unbelieving brethren among the people of the Book, 'If you be driven forth, we will go forth with you; and in what concerneth you, never will we obey any one: and if ye be attacked, we will certainly come to your help.' But God is witness that they are liars.
>
> If they were driven forth, they would not share their banishment; if they were attacked they would not help them, or if they help them they will surely turn their backs.—Súratu'l-Hashr (lix) 11–12.

For the time, however, it put some courage into the hearts of the Bani Naḍír, who sent a message to Muḥammad saying: 'we shall not depart from our possessions; do what thou wilt against us.' This suited the Prophet's plans and, on hearing of their resolve, he said: 'The Jews have resolved to fight', and in a loud voice pronounced the Takbír—'great is the Lord'. His followers also expressed their joy in the same way, and the words Alláhu Akbar, Alláhu Akbar resounded on all sides. Preparations for the conflict were then made, and a force sufficient for the purpose soon set out from Madína. 'Alí, as usual, was the standard bearer. The Bani Naḍír, though they failed to get help from the neighbouring tribes or from the Bani Quraiẓa, made, for a time, a stout resistance, which led Muḥammad to adopt a plan contrary to all the Arab usages of war. He ordered Abú Lailá Mázaní and Muḥammad 'Abdu'lláh bin Sallám to cut down the date trees except the kind called the A'júz.[1] The Jews remonstrated in vain against so unjust a proceeding, which was opposed to the precepts of the Law of Moses,[2] a Law which the Qur'án professed to confirm; but the order went forth that the trees were to be utterly destroyed.

The Bani Naḍír, seeing that further resistance was useless, sent to say that they were ready to abandon their lands, now rendered useless. The siege had lasted about three weeks and Muḥammad was apparently glad to come to terms. He allowed them to go away with their camels and such goods as they could load upon them, except their weapons. These and the crops he divided amongst his followers. The banishment of the Bani Naḍír enabled the Prophet to provide a permanent means of livelihood for the men who came with him from Mecca. At the same time it showed that opposition to his will was becoming powerless, and that the various Jewish tribes would not combine for mutual defence. Thus his prestige greatly increased.

There are a few points of special interest in this affair. The first is the alleged plot by the Bani Naḍír to kill Muḥammad, which is brought

[1] *Mudáriju'n-Nabúwat*, p. 623: but the *Raudatu's-Ṣafá*, part II, vol. ii, p. 420 says that Abú Lailá felled the A'júz trees, saying, 'This will much sadden and distress the Jews': on the other hand, 'Abdu'lláh ibn Salám says that he only cut down the worst, knowing that God would give the best trees to the Muslims.

[2] Deut. xx. 19.

forward as a justification for this Ghazwa. The *Mudáriju'n-Nabúwat* (p. 623) states that, in the interview with the Bani Naḍír, Muḥammad was leaning against a wall, when Ḥuzya ibn Akhtab suggested that a stone should be thrown from the wall upon his head. Wáqidi, who says he gained information from a tradition (ḥadíth), gives a similar account (p. 276). He goes on to say that 'Amru bin Jaḥsh volunteered to do it, but that Sallám bin Mashkam persuaded them not to agree to such a proceeding, and that Gabriel opportunely gave the Prophet intimation of this danger, on which he departed and returned to Madína.

Cherágh 'Alí in the *Critical Exposition of the Jihád* (p. 34) defends the dealing of Muḥammad with the Bani Naḍír and alleges that they made a conspiracy to kill him. He accepts the statements of the traditions on this subject; but when dealing with the affair of Nakhla and when defending the Prophet's action there, he discards the traditional accounts, saying: 'The affair of the Nakhla marauding party, as related in the traditions, is full of discrepancies and is altogether inconsistent and untrustworthy' (p. 30). If then tradition is an unreliable source when telling against Muḥammad, why should it be more reliable when telling against those whom he was seeking to subdue and to dispossess of their property. But he is not even consistent with himself, for later on (p. 109) he says, referring to the alleged crime of their attempt on the life of the Prophet, or their expulsion for the same, that 'the traditions on the subject are unsupported, *ex parte* and legendary'. This is sound historical criticism, worthy of the distinguished author, and is supported by so great an authority as Sir W. Muir who says: 'The evidence is altogether *ex parte*, and cast in the usual mode of fiction.'[1] This statement is further confirmed by the fact that no mention of any such proposal is made in the Qur'án. Cherágh 'Alí says, 'A whole Súra (lix) in the Qur'án is devoted to the Bani Naḍír, but it does not hint at the alleged crime of their attempt on the life of the Prophet.'[2] This excuse for the expulsion of the Jews from their homes must then be set aside, and some other reason be found. That reason is not far to seek.

We have seen that the Muhájirún were poor and dependent on the Anṣár, the inhabitants of Madína. Previous Ghazwas and Sariyas had not brought in much plunder. The lands of the Bani Naḍír were near at hand, and would form a valuable property for the Prophet's needy followers. As a matter of fact, it was, with the exception of some given to two poor men of Madína, all given to the Muhájirún. It is expressly said that this was done to enable them to be independent

[1] *The Life of Mahomet*, vol. iii, p. 210.
[2] *Critical Exposition of the Jihád*, p. 109.

of the support of the Anṣár and that they might have a sufficiency to live upon.[1] This arrangement by which one class alone of his followers gained much benefit needed some justification and so a revelation was produced:—

> To the poor (Muhájirún) doth a part belong, who have been driven from their homes (Mecca) and their substance.—Súratu'l-Hashr (lix) 5.

Another point of interest is the destruction of the date trees. Cherágh 'Alí says,[2] that the trees were neither bearing fruit, nor did they supply any staple article of food and that, therefore, the action was not contrary to the Law of Moses, which says: 'Only the trees which thou knowest that they be not trees for meat, thou shalt destroy and cut them down' (Deut. xx. 20). The destruction is thus referred to in the Qur'án:—

> Your cutting down of their palm trees[3] and sparing others was by God's permission.—Súratu'l-Hashr (lix) 5.

This statement needs some examination. The *Mudáriju'n-Nabúwat* (p. 624) states that there was some doubt in the minds of some Muslims as to the propriety of cutting down date trees, and that then came the revelation permitting it. If the trees were fruitless, it is difficult to see

[1] *Mudáriju'n-Nabúwat*, p. 625.

[2] *Critical Exposition of the Jihád*, p. 110.

[3] The Arabic word is Lína (لينة) and Cherágh 'Alí Ṣáḥib says this is 'a tree without fruit'; but it seems to be an ordinary name for any tree.

why doubts arose. However it goes on to say that there were three kinds of date trees, Lína, 'Ajwa and Barní; that the Prophet only destroyed the Lína which was not used for food, whilst he spared the other two kinds which did produce food. Now this seems to be one of the traditions, which grew up to shield the Prophet. It is untrustworthy, for the *Mudájiru'n-Nabúwat* itself goes on to say that the author of the *Kashsháf* translates Lína simply as 'a date tree'; that Baiḍáwí calls it a 'munificent date tree';[1] another rendering is 'a kind of date tree': the Qámús explains it as 'a kind of date tree, loaded with fruit[2] suitable for food, and adds that the whole matter is not free from confusion and perplexity. It is clear then that Cherágh 'Alí's statement cannot be accepted as a solution of the difficulty.

Other authorities find no perplexity, for Abú Layli felled the most fruitful date trees called 'Ajwa, saying: 'This will sadden and distress the Jews;'[3] but Ibn Sallám felled the worst saying: 'I know that all the property of the Jews will belong to the professors of Islám, and I have, therefore, left the best for them;' so apparently good and bad were destroyed together. Wáqidi says that the dates of the trees destroyed were

1 النخلة الكريمة *Baiḍáwi*, vol. ii, p. 323.

2 دقل, which may mean a bad kind of fruit; still it is fruit.

3 *Násikhu't-Tawárikh*, part I, vol. ii, p. 194.

of a yellow colour, with such a delicate skin and substance that the stone within appeared to view and that they were much liked. Maulawí Naḍír Aḥmad, in his Urdu translation of the Qur'án, renders translates Líwa simply as date trees. There thus seems no sufficient reason for limiting the meaning of Líwa to trees which bear no fruit, and Cherágh 'Alí has not, in this case, used his usual critical skill. Muḥammad evidently felt that he had broken the Mosaic law and departed from Arab usage; otherwise no special revelation would have been needed. The case must be given against him.

THE GHAZWA OF THE LESSER BADR

The next event is called the Ghazwa-i-Badr-i-Mau'id, or the Ghazwa of promise, and the Lesser Badr, an expedition in which no fighting took place. After the victory at Uḥud, Abú Sufyán said to the Muslims: 'We will meet again next year at Badr.' Then by the order of the Prophet, 'Umar Fárúq said: 'Please God.' When the time arrived there was a drought and a scarcity of food, and so Abú Sufyán wished to postpone the conflict. Whether this was the true reason, or whether he found that his victory at Uḥud had not permanently weakened the Prophet's position, it is not easy to say. Anyhow, he sent Nu'aim bin Ma'súd to Madína as a spy, and instructed him to inform the Muslims of the great strength of the Meccan forces. Accordingly he went and in the words of the 'Rauḍatu'ṣ-Ṣafá' said: 'It will be better for you to withdraw your feet within the skirts of security and not to leave Madína on any account.' The Muslims were afraid to go forth; but Abú Bakr and 'Umar, ever ready for any deed of daring, persuaded the Prophet to give orders for the expedition. Muḥammad did so, saying: 'I swear by that God in the power of whose grasp my life is, that we shall sally forth, even if not a single individual accompanies us.' He took with him fifteen hundred men, a force double the size of any he had ever before taken. He carried much merchandise for sale at the fair, where they waited for eight days for the Quraish attack. Abú Sufyán started out with a force of two thousand and fifty men, but after two or three days had to return for want of provender. The Muslims having sold their goods to advantage returned to Madína. Muḥammad was highly pleased at the result, and produced a revelation showing the divine approval of the affair:—

> As to those who after the reverse [1] which befell them respond to God and His Apostle—such of them as do good works and fear God, shall have a great reward.
>
> Who, when men said to them, 'Now are the Meccans mustering against you; therefore fear them', it only

[1] At Uḥud.

> increased their faith, and they said, 'Our sufficiency is God and He is an excellent Protector.'
>
> They returned, therefore, with the favour of God, enriched by him, and untouched by harm; and they followed what was well pleasing to God, and God is of great munificence.
>
> Verily that devil[1] would cause you to fear his friends: but fear them not, but fear me, if ye are believers.—Suratu Ali 'Imran (iii) 166–9.

For some time after this no Ghazwa or Sariya of any importance took place, and the summer and autumn months of the fourth year of the Hijra passed in peace. The Prophet had now leisure to attend to his domestic affairs, but an account of these lies outside the scope of this book.

In the beginning of the fifth year of the Hijra (May A.D. 626), there were a few small expeditions against certain Jewish tribes. It was on one of these that the Ṣalátu'l-Khauf, or prayer of fear, was instituted. In order to guard against a surprise, a part of the force was kept under arms, when the rest were saying the Ṣalát, the prescribed prayers, which were curtailed in accordance with the revelation:—

> When ye go forth to war in the land, it shall be no crime in you to cut short your prayers, if ye fear lest the infidel come upon you . . . let a party of them

1 Baiḍáwí says that this refers to Nu'aim or to Abú Sufyán; he also says that the words 'fear me' mean 'fear to disobey my commands, fight with my apostle'. vol. i, p. 186.

rise up with thee, but let them take their arms; and when they shall have made their prostrations, let them retire to your rear: then let another party that hath not prayed come forward and let them pray with you.—Suratu'n-Nisa' (iv) 102-3.[1]

GHAZWA OF THE BANI MUSTALIQ

A few months later the Ghazwa of the Baní Musṭaliq took place. Their chief, al-Ḥárith bin Abi Ḍarár, had persuaded several other tribes to join together for a raid on Madína. Muḥammad hearing of this sent a spy, named Barida, into their camp. He promised to bring assistance to them and being allowed to depart in order to fetch it, he went straight to the Prophet and gave the needed information. The Prophet then set forth with a considerable force containing thirty horsemen, and determined to defeat the object of the enemy by a previous attack on them. 'Alí was the standard bearer and 'Umar binu'l-Khaṭṭáb led the van. A large part of the Munáfiqún, the dissatisfied people of Madína, joined the force, led, it is said, by 'the hope of plunder and worldly considerations'[2] to do so, which clearly shows what was the expected results of these raids. This one resulted in a complete victory for the Muslims. Two thousand camels

1 For details as to the ritual of this Ṣalát, see *The Faith of Islám* (3rd ed.) p. 314.

2 *Mudáriju'n-Nabúwat*, p. 630.

and many flocks of sheep and goats were captured. Two hundred families were taken prisoners and taken to Madína. Juwaira, the daughter of al-Ḥáriṯẖ, despairing of finding the ransom fixed by her captor, appealed to the Prophet. 'Áyesha describes her as very beautiful and graceful.[1] Muḥammad listened to her story, proposed marriage to her and was accepted. The people then looked upon the Baní Musṭaliq as relatives, and set all the prisoners free, on which 'Áyesha declared that 'no woman was ever such a blessing to her people as Juwaira'. The division of the booty led to an altercation between the men of Madína and the Mahájirún. The Prophet settled it with some difficulty. The occasion led to the delivery of the Súratu'l-Munáfiqún (lxiii). The Munáfiqún, or hypocrites, were dissatisfied with the growing power of Muḥammad in temporal affairs, and this Súra is a severe indictment of their conduct. Their opposition gradually died away.

Another event of some interest took place on the return march. It is known as the slander about 'Áyesha. The simplest method of settling the claims of his many wives to accompany him on these expeditions led Muḥammad to devise the plan of doing it by drawing lots. In this case 'Áyesha was the favoured wife. On the return

[1] زنی بود بسیار شیرین و ملیح و صاحب حسن و جمال *Mudáriju'n-Nabúwat*, p. 631.

journey, according to her own account, she stayed behind to find a bracelet, and her bearers thinking she was inside her litter went on without her. In her distress she wrapped her clothes around her and sat down. After a while, one of the men, Ṣafwán binu'l-Mu'aṭṭah, found her and brought her to Madína. This was a very simple affair, though the fact that 'Áyesha had stated that on seeing Juwaira the 'fire of envy arose in her heart'[1] may have given rise to suspicion about her conduct. The scandal-mongers took it up, hoping to put the Prophet in the dilemma of either offending Abú Bakr, his father-in-law, or of damaging his position by condoning the offence. After her return 'Áyesha fell sick and retired to her father's house. For some weeks the Prophet remained away. The whole affair was troublesome, but the usual opportune revelation came and one day the Prophet went to see her and said: 'O 'Áyesha rejoice, Verily the Lord hath revealed thine innocence.' The opening verses of the Súratu'n-Núr (xxiv) were then delivered to the people, and 'Áyesha's character was cleared, and some of her calumniators received the punishment prescribed in the verse:—

> Those who defame virtuous women and bring not four witnesses scourge them with fourscore stripes.[2]

[1] *Mudáriju'n-Nabúwat*, p. 631.

[2] The whole story, is given in the *Mudáriju'n-Nabúwat*, in the *Rauḍatu's-Ṣafá*, and in the *Násikhu't-Tuwárikh*, and very

GHAZWA OF THE DITCH

We now come to the Ghazwa-i-Khandaq (ditch) or as it is also called the Ghazwa-i-Aḥzáb (confederates) in the fifth year of the Hijra. It came about in this way. Muḥammad's treatment of the Baní Naḍír soon produced reprisals on their part. They were dispersed in various towns, and not finding sufficient energy amongst the Jewish tribes to combine for the defence of their homes and property, some of them who lived at Khaibar turned to the Quraish leaders in Mecca, and expressed a wish to form an alliance with them. Abú Sufyán welcomed their assistance, and, after recounting what he considered to be the good points of the Quraish religion and practice, asked the Jews whether the Quraish or the Muslims were the better people. The story goes that the Jews, though they hated idolatry, gave preference to the Quraish over the orthodox religion and most noble law on account of their envy, not dreading the wrath of God, who thereupon revealed this verse[1]:—

> Hast thou not observed those to whom a part of the Scriptures hath been given? They believe in al-Jibt and al-Taghut and say of the infidels, 'These are guided to a better path than those who hold the faith. These

fully with useful notes in Muir's *Life of Mohamet*, vol. iii, pp. 244–54.

[1] *Rauḍatu's-Ṣafá*, part II, vol. ii, p. 443.

are they whom God hath cursed.'—Suratu'n-Nisa' (iv) 54-5.

The next step was to enlist the aid of the Baní Ghaṭafán, to whom the Jews promised one year's crop of dates. The aid of other Arab tribes was also secured, and Abú Sufyán found himself at the head of 10,000 men, and the siege of Madína soon commenced. The defeat at Uḥud had taught the Muslims caution, and at a meeting of the Muhájirún and the Anṣár it was decided to act on the defensive. Salmán, the Persian, stated that in Persia the defenders of a town dug a deep ditch around it, and suggested that it should be done here and now. This happy suggestion was adopted, and the compact nature of the stone houses which formed a wall, and the ditch, which filled up the vacant space, proved an excellent protection. It took six days to complete the defences which were made before the enemy arrived. As the weather was cold and the ground was hard, the digging of the ditch was very difficult. To encourage his men Muḥammad himself took part in the work and sang: 'O Lord, there is no happiness but that of futurity, wherefore have mercy on the Anṣár and the Muhájirún.' To which his men replied: 'Unto Muḥammad we have pledged our faith to fight his foes and flee not until death.' Muḥammad was then on good terms with the Jews of Baní Quraiẓa, who lent the necessary spades, baskets and other tools for the work.[1] The Quraish had never seen anything so contrary to Arab modes of warfare before and were quite disconcerted. A few horsemen one day got over a weak part, but being entirely unsupported they were successfully repulsed, and two of their number were slain. One of them 'Amr bin 'Abdud was slain by 'Alí in single combat. Tradition states that they fought from morn till eve, when 'Alí suddenly exclaimed: 'See thy brother is coming behind thee.' 'Amr looked round and thus gave 'Alí the opportunity he sought for of slaying his opponent.

The work in the trenches was heavy and incessant, and though the Quraish did not again attempt to force their way over it, the Muslims were weary with their incessant watch and began to murmur. This is referred to the verses:—

> When they assailed you from above you and from below you, and when your eyes became distracted, and your hearts came up into your throats, and ye thought diverse thoughts, Then were the faithful tried, and with strong quaking did they quake.—Suratu'l-Ahzab (xxxiii) 10-11.

The people doubting his promise of divine aid wished to retire from the outer defensive works into the city. They were thus rebuked by a revelation:—

> When the disaffected and the diseased of heart said God and His Apostle have made us but a cheating promise.

1 *Násikhu't-Tawáríkh*, part I, vol. ii, p. 215.

And when a party of them said, 'O men of Yethrib (Madina). This is no place of safety for you here; therefore return into the city.' And another party of you asked the Prophet's leave to return saying, 'our houses are defenceless'. No! they were not left defenceless, but their sole thought was to flee away.

Say, flight shall not profit you.—Suratu'l-Ahzab. (xxxiii). 12–13, 16.

Muḥammad then resorted to a successful stratagem which spread discord amongst his opponents. Food and forage also were giving out, the weather suddenly became cold and boisterous and so, after carrying on the siege for fifteen days, Abú Sufyán gave the order to depart and Madína was safe. It was a notable victory for the Muslims who lost only five men. It was the last serious conflict Muḥammad had with the Quraish.

This Ghazwa is of interest on account of the intrigues carried on by all parties, and in the sad result to which it led—the massacre of the Baní Quraiẕa Jews. These men at first aided Muḥammad by supplying tools for the excavation of the ditch, but Abú Sufyán deceived them, and detached them from their allegiance to the Prophet, lukewarm as it very naturally may have been, for the time for trusting the Prophet has passed away. He sent a Jewish chief, Huyay bin Akhṭab, to impress them with the danger they were in, and promised to give them armed support to defend their fort if attacked. After a long debate they were persuaded to give up their treaty with Muḥammad. They do not appear to have taken any active part in the conflict and failed to assist the Quraish when called upon to do so. Muḥammad then tried to detach the Arabs of the Baní Ghaṭafán from their union with the Quraish by offering a bribe of one-third of the produce of Madína, but some of his followers objected to this arrangement and it fell through.

Very soon after this, a man named Nu'ím bin Ma'súd Ghaṭafání, waited on the Prophet and expressed his desire to help him and his wish to embrace Islám. Muḥammad said: 'Art thou able to throw discord among the infidels and to destroy their league?' He said: 'I can; but thou must allow me to speak whatever I like.' His lordship permitted him to do so and dismissed him with these words: 'War is a deception.'[1] Nu'ím then tried to persuade the Jews that the Quraish were playing them false, and advised them to require Abú Sufyán to deliver some hostages to them as a sign of good faith. He then visited the Quraish and told them that he had secret information that the Jews intended to keep faith with Muḥammad and were not to be relied upon, that they would ask for hostages and then deliver them up to death. Thus doubt

1 *Rauḍatu's-Ṣafá*, part II, vol. ii, p. 459.

arose in Abú Sufyán's mind. He sent a message to the Jews for assistance in an attack the next day; but they said they could not fight on the Sabbath. This confirmed the suspicion and, as the sequel shows, the Quraish notwithstanding a previous promise did nothing to protect them.[1]

GHAZWA OF THE BANI QURAIZA

The raising of the siege of Madína was followed by the Ghazwa of the Baní Quraiẕa. In the figurative language of the oriental chronicler, 'when the breeze of divine favour, which wafted only from the spirit of Alláh, commenced to blow and the morn of prosperity began to dawn in the orient of hope, the adherents of rebellion and sin, whose head and chief was Abú Sufyán, returned overthrown.' The victors won, Gabriel appeared to Muḥammad and told him not to put off his arms for the angels had not done so for forty days, and he gave a direct command: 'O Muḥammad, arise to strike the idolaters who are possessors of the book, the Baní Quraiẕa. By Alláh I am going to batter their fort and to break it to pieces like the egg of a hen cast against a stone'.[2] Muḥammad obeyed and gave the order

[1] The whole story of this intrigue is given in the *Mudáriju'n-Nabúwat*, pp. 646–7.

[2] This fact about Gabriel is related by all the historians, and seems to show that even they felt the need of some very definite justification for so great a massacre which followed.

for the immediate march of an army of three thousand men, with 'Alí as the standard bearer. The fortress was soon invested and the Jews, who seem to have laid in no stock of provision for a siege, quickly found themselves in great distress. After fifteen days or so had elapsed they requested permission to emigrate as the Baní Naḍír had done. This was refused. They then offered to leave all their goods and chattels behind. The reply was that they must surrender unconditionally. Then their leaders, Ka'b bin Asud and Huyay bin Akhṭab, gathered the Jews together and put three courses of action before them. First, that they should accept Islám. They replied that they could not change their religion. Second, that they should kill the women and children, go forth and fight to the death. They said they could not kill innocent beings and that they would have no happiness in their own lives after such a loss. Third, to fight on the Sabbath when the Muslims would not expect an attack and would be off their guard. They declined to violate the Sabbath.

The Jews then asked that Abú Labába might come and advise them. He said they must capitulate, but overcome by the weeping and wailing of the women and children, put his hand across

In the *Mudáriju'n-Nabúwat* (p. 650) it is said: 'The order of God was to go against the Baní Quraiẓa.' It is also said that 'Gabriel appeared and gave the order.'

his throat to signify that death was before them and thus encouraged them to resist. At last, when starvation was before them, the Jews capitulated, and turning to their allies[1], the Baní Aws, said: 'Why do you not help us as the Baní Khazraj helped the Qainuqá?' Then the Baní Aws pleaded with Muḥammad for mercy for their friends, who had repented of their breach of faith; but all he would consent to was that one of their number should decide the case. Assuming that he would choose one of the men then present, who were acquainted with all the facts of the case, they agreed to this, then *he himself chose* the umpire in the person of Sa'd bin Mu'ádh,[2]

1 حلفاء or احلاف pl. of حليف an ally.

2 *Rauḍatu'ṣ-Ṣafá*, part II, vol. ii, p. 475.

See also *Mudáriju'n-Nabúwat* (p. 653), where it is said that Muḥammad took no notice of the petition of the Baní Aws and himself sent for Sa'd. The following is the statement in Persian:—

حضرت در معامله اوسیان هیچ نفرمود و تغافل زد پس فرستاد کسی را بطلب سعد بن معاذ که بسبب جراحت ازان غزوه تخلف نموده بود .

'His Excellency gave no order in the matter of the Baní Aws and showed negligence: then he sent some one to call Sa'd bin Mu'ádh who, on account of wounds received in this Ghazwa, had been left behind.'

The exact words of the *Rauḍatu'ṣ-Ṣafá* are 'His Lordship, however, made no reply to the Baní Aws, till their solicitations exceeded all bounds when he asked: "Will you agree that one of yourselves make a decision concerning them?" They said: "Yes, O Apostle of God." He continued: "That man will be Sa'd bin Mu'ádh." We shall do whatever he decides in this matter' (part II, vol. ii, p. 475).

formerly a friend of the Jews, but having been wounded in a recent skirmish was now vexed with them for not having rendered assistance to the Muslims[1] and who was not then present. With such a man for an umpire, the decision was a foregone conclusion. Gabriel's order was clear and it is extremely unlikely that Muḥammad ever intended it to be set aside. He knew his man and that the issue was safe in his hands.

The author of the well-known history, Násikhu't-Tawáríkh, (part I, vol. ii, p. 237) thus states the case:—

اشراف از قبیلهٔ اوس درحضرت پیغمبر انبوه شدند و عرض کردند یهودی
بنی قینقاع را بمردم خزرج بخشیدی روا باشد که بنی قریظه را بما بخشی
رسول خدای فرمود هیچ رضا هستید که از میان شما مردی اختیار کنم
و او را حکم سازم و بدانچه درمیان ایشان حکومت کند بپردازم گفتند
آری یا رسول الله فرمود آن مرد سعد بن معاذ است .

'The principal men from the tribe of the Bani Aws came to the Prophet and said: "You pardoned the Baní Qainuqá at the intercession of the Khazraj. It is right that at our intercession you should pardon the Baní Quraiẓa." The Prophet replied: "Do you agree that I should choose a man from among yourselves and make him an umpire and should carry out what he orders in the matter." They said: "Yes, O Apostle of God." He replied: "That man is Sa'd bin Muá'dh."'

It is clear that they thought he would choose one of those who were present as umpire, not send off to Madína to fetch a man who had not been present at their interview, had not heard the reasons given for showing mercy, and who was smarting from his wounds.

[1] It is said that on being wounded he cursed the Baní Quraiẓa and prayed thus: 'O Lord, suffer me not to die until my heart hath had its revenge upon them.' Muir's *Life of Maḥomet*, vol. iii, p. 274, and the *Musnad* iii, pp. 350, 363 quoted by Margoliouth, *Moḥammad*, p. 332.

The men of the Baní Aws said to Sa'd: 'The Apostle of God has left to thy option the judgement concerning the Baní Quraiẓa. They are thy friends, who have aided thee in peace and in war. They have surrendered everything and now their only hope centres in thee.' With many such like words they urged him to be merciful. He put them off with an ambiguous speech, and expressed a wish to know whether they would abide by his judgement. No other course was open and so they agreed, nothing doubting but like them he would abide by the recognized position of a ḥalíf or ally. The Baní Aws had behaved so well all through and with such loyalty to their friends, that it is impossible to suppose that they ever thought that Sa'd could possibly betray the allies (aḥláf) of his own tribe.

All being now ready the seven or eight hundred prisoners, with their arms bound behind them, stood on the one side; on the other were the women and the children in dread terror of coming events. Muḥammad took up his position in front with his chief followers. Sa'd, a big burly man, now wearied with his journey and smarting from his wounds stands by. 'Proceed with thy judgement,' said the Prophet. Then came from a revengeful man these cruel words: 'This verily is my judgement, that the male captives shall be put to death, that the female captives and the children shall be sold into slavery, and the spoil be divided among the army.' Any murmuring at this savage decree was at once stayed by Muḥammad who said: 'Truly thou hast decided according to the judgement of God pronounced on high from beyond the seven heavens.' The men were then taken to Madína. Muḥammad ordered a trench to be dug. The next day the Jews were brought forth in batches, and 'Alí and Zubair were directed to slay them. Darkness came on before 'Alí and Zubair had completed their bloody task. Torches were then brought to give light for the completion of this cruel deed. The blood of nearly eight hundred men flowed into the ditch, on the brink of which the victims were made to kneel. Muḥammad looked on with approval, and when Huyay bin Akhṭab was brought before him said: 'O enemy of God, at last the Most High has given thee into my hands and has made me thy judge.'[1] Some of the females were divided amongst the Muslims and the rest were sold as slaves. A beautiful widow, whose husband had just been slaughtered, was reserved by Muḥammad for his own ḥarem.

Thus, when two tribes had been exiled and one exterminated, the power of the Jews was broken for ever in Madína, and Muḥammad was free to look farther afield for fresh conquests. There

[1] *Rauḍatu's-Ṣafá*, part II, vol. ii, p. 477. This shows that Muḥammad accepted responsibility for the judgement given by Ka'b.

was a time when he had desired their friendship, but each victory won and each lot of booty captured made him less dependent on them for recognition and for funds. 'The change from a basis of reason to a basis of force had taken place gradually, but was now finally achieved.'[1]

After the whole affair was over, Muḥammad recited as a revelation from God the following statement now recorded in Súratu'l-Aḥzáb (xxiii) 9–28:—

> O believers! remember the goodness of God towards you, when the armies came against you, and we sent against them a blast, and hosts that ye saw not; for the eye of God was upon your doings:
>
> When they assailed you from above you, and from below you, and when your eyes became distracted, and your hearts came up into your throat, and ye thought divers thoughts of God:
>
> Then were the faithful tried, and with strong quaking did they quake:
>
> And when the disaffected and the diseased of heart said, 'God and his Apostle have made us but a cheating promise:'
>
> And when a party of them said, 'O people of Yathrib! there is no place of safety for you here; therefore return *into the city*.' And another party of you asked the Prophet's leave to return, saying, 'Our houses are left defenceless.' No! they were not left defenceless: but their sole thought was to flee away.
>
> If the enemy had effected an entry at all points, and they (the disaffected) had been asked to promote

[1] Margoliouth, *Moḥammad*, p. 334.

confusion, they would have done so; but only a short time would they have remained in it.

They had before pledged themselves to God that they would not turn their backs; and a pledge given to God must be enquired of.

SAY: Flight shall not profit you; if ye have fled the death or the slaughter, yet even then, but a little while shall ye enjoy *your good things!*

SAY: Who is he that will screen you from God, whether He choose to bring evil on you, or to shew you mercy? None beside God shall they find to be their patron or helper.

God well knoweth those among you who cause hindrances, and those who say to their brethren, 'Come hither to us;' and who come not to the fight except a little.

It is out of covetousness in your regard: for when an alarm cometh, thou mayest see them look to thee, and roll their eyes like him on whom the shadows of death have fallen! Yet, when the alarm is passed, with sharp tongues will they assail you, covetous of the best of the spoil. No faith have these! God will make their doings of no avail! And easy is this with God.

They thought that the confederates would never retire: and were the confederates to come again, they would fain be dwelling among the Arabs of the desert, *and there* ask news about you! for though they were with you, they fought not except a little.

A noble pattern had ye in God's Apostle, for all who hope in God, and in the latter day, and oft remember God!

And when the faithful saw the confederates, they said, 'This is what God and His Apostle promised us, and God and His Apostle spoke truly:' and it only increased their faith and self-devotion.

Some were there among the faithful who made good what they had promised to God. Some have fulfilled their course, and others await *its fulfilment*, and have not been changelings who change—

That God may reward the faithful for their faithfulness, and may punish the hypocrites, if He so please, or be turned unto them: for God is Forgiving, Merciful.

And God drove back the infidels in their wrath; they won no advantage; God sufficed the faithful in the fight: for God is Strong, Mighty!

And He caused those of the people of the Book (the Jews), who had aided *the confederates*, to come down out of their fortresses, and cast dismay into their hearts: some ye slew, others ye took prisoners.

And He gave you their land, and their dwellings, and their wealth, for an heritage—even a land on which ye had never set foot: for the might of God is equal to all things.

Modern Muslim writers evidently feel that this slaughter of the Jews requires some explanation, though to the older historians it was sufficient that Gabriel appeared, and gave the order to 'strike the idolaters who are possessors of the book'.[1]

Maulaví Cherágh 'Alí says that the Baní Quraiẓa 'instead of co-operating with the Muslims, defected from their allegiance and entered into negotiations with the besieging foe. After the cessation of the siege, they were besieged in turn, and a fearful example of them was made, not by Muḥammad, but by an arbiter chosen and appointed by themselves . . . they were war-

[1] *Ante*, p. 44 and footnote.

traitors and rebels and deserved death according to the international law.'[1]

We have seen how the Jews were deceived both by the Meccans and the Muslims, how at first they rendered assistance in the defence, by the loan of the necessary tools, though as the siege progressed they gave no further aid; we have seen that the arbiter was chosen not by themselves, but by Muḥammad who selected, not one of the Baní Aws who were present and who had pleaded for mercy, but one who was already embittered against the Jews, and who had to be brought from Madína for this purpose.

Again, it was not the Jews who agreed to abide by Sa'd's decision, but the Baní Aws, which is quite another matter. They appealed to Sa'd to have mercy. Sa'd replied to them: 'Do you make an agreement and promise before the Lord Most High that you will assent to my decision and will not transgress it?' They all answered affirmatively.[2]

Maulaví Cherágh 'Alí further says that Muḥammad disapproving the judgement remarked to Sa'd: 'Thou hast decided like the decision of a

[1] *Critical Exposition of Jihád*, pp. 87–8.

[2] The *Rauḍatu'ṣ-Ṣafá* (part II, vol. ii, p. 476), the *Mudáriju'n-Nabúwat* (p. 654) and the *Násikhu't-Tawáríkh* (part I, vol. ii, p. 237) give a statement, showing conclusively that it was the Baní Aws who agreed to accept the decision of an arbiter, whom Muḥammad himself then chose. They, not the Jews, left it in his hands, and he decided whom to appoint.

king, meaning thereby a despotic monarch'.[1] The inference drawn from the use of the word king (Málik) that Muḥammad looked upon it as a despotic act is ingenious; but it would be quite as lawful to assume that he looked upon it as a just one, for kings do not necessarily give despotic opinions. Nor is the interpretation borne out by the subsequent action of Muḥammad, who was not at all the man to do the bidding of another, if he disapproved of it; nor is it in accordance with the historical accounts. Thus, the Apostle of God then exclaimed: 'Sa'd thou hast judged them as God the Most High and Glorious hath judged them from the height of the seventh heaven.'[2] The Right Honourable Syed Amír 'Alí, who, in all such matters, plays rather the part of an advocate with a brief to defend a case, rather than that of an accurate historian, also deals with this subject.[3] He does not record the fact that the Baní Quraiẓa did assist in the preparation

1 *Critical Exposition of Jihád*, p. 138. Some authors have the word Malak (angel) meaning thereby Gabriel, others say Málik (king) is used metaphorically for God (see ibid. p. 38, and the *Mudáriju'n-Nabúwat*, p. 654). These authorities show that Muḥammad did approve of and confirm the verdict. I accept the view of Maulaví Cherágh 'Alí that the word king is used in its ordinary sense, though I do not consider that his deduction therefrom is a sound one.

2 *Rauḍatu'ṣ-Ṣafá*, part II, vol. ii, p. 476. The *Mudáriju'n-Nabúwat* (p. 658) also clearly shows that before Sa'd gave the order, Muḥammad knew that the order would be in accordance with God's will, and that he knew this by inspiration (ilhám).

3 The *Life and Teachings of Moḥammed*, pp. 168–74.

of the defence by lending tools, nor does he show that they made any active opposition. He states, though he gives no authorities for it, that the Jews made the condition that Sa'd should judge the matter, but as we have shown, it was the Bání Aws who made that arrangement. His description of Sa'd is historically accurate. 'This man, a fierce soldier who had been wounded in the attack, and indeed, died from his wounds the next day, infuriated by their treacherous conduct, gave sentence that the fighting men should be put to death and that the women and children should become the slaves of the Moslems.' It is absolutely incredible that the Jews would have chosen such a man to decide their fate, and this leads the student, who has a true historical judgement, to look upon the account given by the older historians as the more probable one.

It is quite fair to urge the plea that we must not judge the actions of ordinary men of a barbarous age by the principles recognized by our own age, but the claim is that Muḥammad was not an ordinary man, but a divinely commissioned teacher, acting under divine guidance. It may also be said that in the Jewish history of the past savage deeds were done, which we should now disapprove; that the persecution of the Jews by the emperor Heraclius in the year A.D. 630 was as bad as this massacre. But there is this difference: no one justifies the cruelty of the Roman emperor, nor are his actions taken as precedents which must be followed by all good Christians. On the other hand, the actions of Muḥammad were, as Muslims must believe, done under supernatural guidance, and they form a definite rule of faith—the Sunna to which all Muḥammadans must conform. His actions, therefore, cannot be justified by comparison with the actions of other men. They belong to a different category; they are, according to Muslim theology, the result of a divine impulse within him, the deeds of a sinless and, therefore, perfect man. They form the highest ideal and the most perfect conception of life which Islám can present. All apologies for Muḥammad based on the fact that other leaders, religious or secular, have done similar deeds are beside the question altogether.

The events of the sixth year of the Hijra (beginning A.D. May 28, 627) have been thus described: 'The whole of the sixth year was occupied with expeditions in which sometimes Muḥammad himself, but more often Abú 'Ubaida, 'Alí and Zaid took the command. They were ordinarily, though not invariably, successful; and the restless energy of the Prophet spread the fame of Islám over a constantly widening area and won for it the respect which success inspires.'[1] We

[1] Margoliouth, *Moḥammed*, p. 339.

need not linger over these raids and conflicts,[1] but there are two events which may be briefly noticed.

SARIYA OF ZAID BIN HARITHA

In the month of Ramaḍán Zaid ibn Ḥáritha was placed in charge of a mercantile caravan with instructions to proceed to Syria. The Muslims, now adepts at waylaying caravans, found that other people could do the same, for this caravan was plundered by the Baní Fazára. The traders at Madína were annoyed and Zaid was sent with a strong party to punish the robbers. Their stronghold was captured and Umm Qiriya, an old woman, a person of some influence in her tribe, was cruelly put to death. Her legs were tied to camels, which were then driven in opposite directions, until she was torn asunder. Zaid on his return gave an account of his expedition to Muḥammad who embraced and kissed him.[2] It is not recorded that he expressed disapprobation of this cruel deed.

THE SARIYA OF 'ARNIYYA

The other event was this, a few men of the Baní 'Arníyya had become Muslims. The climate of Madína did not suit these children of the desert, and so Muḥammad kindly allowed them

1 A full account will be found in Muir's *Life of Mahomet*, vol. iv, pp. 1-21.

2 *Mudáriju'n-Nabúwat*, p. 668.

to go forth with one of his herds of milch camels and live in the open air. They regained strength and then tried to run away with the camels. The herdsman who pursued them was cruelly tortured to death, Muḥammad was very naturally angry, and when the culprits were captured and brought before him, he ordered that their eyes should be put out, their arms and legs be cut off and their bodies impaled until life was extinct. It must, however, be stated that Muḥammad seems to have felt that such torture in judicial punishments was not right, for he delivered the following revelation:—

> The recompense of those who war against God and His Apostle, and go about to commit disorders on the earth, shall be that they be slain or crucified, or have their alternate hands and feet cut off, or be banished the land.—Suratu'l-Ma'ida (v) 37.

Impaling is, therefore, now illegal, though the lawful punishments are still inhuman. Unfortunately they are now enshrined in what Muslim law accepts as a divine code.

THE GHAZWA OF HUDAIBIYA

The next event of importance is the attempt to make a pilgrimage to the Ka'ba in Mecca. It resulted in a treaty favourable to the Muslims, which was looked upon as a victory, and so, though no actual fighting took place, the event is called the Ghazwa of Ḥudaibiya. Six years had now passed away since Muḥammad and his followers had left Mecca. The breach with the Jews was complete. The Qibla, or direction in which prayer should be made, was no longer Jerusalem, for Mecca had been substituted for it. No one could expect to be the sole ruler in Arabia who neglected its sacred city and shrine. It was time now to take some account of Arab sentiment and to conciliate the Bedouin tribes. The way was prepared by the revelation of considerable portions of the Súratu'l Ḥajj [(xxii) vv. 27–39; 76–7]. Then when the time for the lesser pilgrimage in the month of Dhu'l-Qa'ida, came round, Muḥammad set forth with a company of about fifteen hundred men. This large force naturally alarmed the Meccans who prepared to resist it by force. The Muslims halted at Ḥudaibiya. As their position was one of some danger, Muḥammad gathered them around himself under the shadow of a tree, and required a pledge of loyalty even to death from each one. The oath was given, and the 'pledge of the tree' is an event ever after referred to with great respect and regard. God is said to have been pleased with it:—

> Well pleased now hath God been with the believers when they plighted fealty to thee under the tree.—Suratu'l-Fath (xlviii) 18.

The Muslims were not allowed to enter Mecca, but war was to be suspended for ten years, and in the following year Muḥammad and his followers were to be allowed to spend three days in Mecca, provided they laid aside the weapons of warriors. The Muslims were greatly disappointed at not being allowed to make the pilgrimage, but Muḥammad raised their spirits by declaring that this treaty was in reality a victory. His followers would probably have found some difficulty in accepting that view, and so he produced a revelation to support his statement:—

> Verily we have won for thee an undoubted victory.—Suratu'l-Fath (xlviii) 1.

In one respect, at least, it was a gain, for the Quraish in treating him as an equal acknowledged his political status.[1] It has been said: 'Each time the Prophet had failed, or secured an incomplete success, he compensated for it by an attack on the Jews. This policy had served too well to be abandoned after the unsatisfactory affair of Ḥudaibiya, and, therefore, a raid on the Jews of Khaibar was speedily planned.'[2]

THE GHAZWA OF KHAIBAR

So we now come to the Ghazwa of Khaibar.

[1] For a fuller historical account of this event, see Muir's *Life of Mahomet*, vol. iv, chapter xix; and for critical remarks on the revelations connected with it, Sell's *Historical Development of the Qur'án* (3rd ed.), pp. 175–83.

[2] Margoliouth, *Moḥammed*, p. 355.

In the revelation given to justify the concluding the treaty of Ḥudaibiya, these words occur:—

> God promised you the taking of a rich booty.—Suratu'l-Fath (xlviii) 20.

According to the great commentator Baiḍáwí this refers to the spoils to be obtained at Khaibar. If this interpretation is correct, it shows that Muḥammad had clearly defined in his own mind the object of this attack on the Jews. He set forth with an army of sixteen hundred men, including a considerable force of cavalry. The valley of Khaibar was a very fertile one. It contained a number of villages, protected by fortresses built in strong positions. By forced marches Muḥammad took the Jews by surprise. They hurriedly sought aid from a friendly tribe of Arabs—the Baní Ghaṭafán, but the Muslims skilfully interposed their force between the Ghaṭafán and Khaibar, and so effectually prevented the union of the two forces. This move was successful, but the historians say the Ghaṭafán heard a voice from heaven saying, 'all that is in your houses will be plundered' and so they returned to their abodes. This, says one historian, was one of the miracles of the Prophet. The siege lasted for some time, and on the whole the Jews made a good defence, but in the end had to yield to superior force. There were as usual single combats in which 'Alí distinguished himself.

Kinána, the chief of the Jews, being accused of misleading Muḥammad about the concealment of treasure, was according to some accounts cruelly tortured and then beheaded.[1] The booty obtained was very great. One half of the land was reserved for Muḥammad and the other half, divided into one thousand eight hundred portions, was reserved for his followers. Those inhabitants, who, after being thus dispossessed of their property, wished to remain, were allowed to do so in order to cultivate the lands, on condition of giving up one half of the produce to the new owner. The 'Rauḍatu'ṣ-Ṣafá' (part II, vol. ii, p. 549) thus describes the conditions on which they remained: 'The inhabitants of Khaibar represented, however, with tears and lamentations, that the professors of Islám would stand in need of men for the cultivation of their gardens and fields. They then offered to work as hirelings in the just-mentioned pursuits without meddling at all with the government. His holy and prophetic lordship accordingly took pity on them, and ordered them to cultivate the fields and vineyards of that region, on condition of paying one half of the proceeds thereof into the public treasury, and retaining the other half for their wages.'

1 Muir's *Life of Mahomet*, vol. iv, p. 68; Margoliouth, *Moḥammed*, p. 360 footnote; but the *Mudáriju'n-Nabúwat* and the *Raudatu's-Ṣafá* made no mention of the torture, and the Right Honourable Syed Amír 'Alí thinks the charge false.

The Jews of Khaibar thus became the first Dhimmís. They held this position until the Khalífa 'Umar ruthlessly drove them from their homes.

Immediately after the death of Kinána, Muḥammad sent for his widow, Ṣafiyya, a woman of great beauty. Her father had perished in the massacre of the Baní Quraiẓa, and her husband now. Notwithstanding, she consented to the marriage which was arranged with undue haste.[1] Maulaví Cherágh 'Alí defends the siege of Khaibar on the ground that it was part of a purely defensive policy, and that it was thus necessary to crush the Jews.[2] He passes over altogether the promise of loot given in Súratu'l-Fatḥ (xlviii. 20–1). Khaibar was, at least, one hundred miles away from Madína, so the danger of any attack from it was very small. Assassins had been sent to Khaibar to kill Abú Ráfi', who is also called Sallám ibn Abú'l-Haqíq, and had succeeded in their object. The murdered man was the brother of Kinána.[3] Two large Jewish tribes had been banished from their homes and one had been exterminated. It would have been a marvel, indeed, if the Jews of Khaibar had been loyal. Anyhow, as the sequel shows, their rich lands and possessions

[1] Muir's *Life of Mahomet*, p. 69 footnote.
[2] *Critical Exposition of Jihád*, p. 39.
[3] The story is given in full in the *Muddáriju'n-Nabúwat*, p. 575, and in the *Rauḍatu's-Ṣafá*, part II, vol. i, pp. 362–4.

were a temptation too strong to be resisted. Margoliouth thus sums up the position:—

'The taking of Khaibar marks the stage at which Islám became a menace to the world. . . . The people of Khaibar, all that distance from Madína, had certainly done him (Muḥammad) and his followers no wrong; for their leaving unavenged the murder of one of their number by his emissary was no act of aggression. 'Alí, when told to lead the forces against them, had to ask for what he was fighting: and was told that he must compel them to accept the formulae of Islám ('Muslim' ii, 237). Khaibar was attacked, because there was booty to be acquired there, and the plea for attacking it was that its inhabitants were *not Moslems*. That plea would cover attacks on the whole world outside Madína.'[1]

Muḥammad returned to Madína after the capture of Khaibar, and passed the autumn and winter of the seventh year of the Hijra quietly at home. He was in no danger now of any attack by the Quraish, and so he occupied his men in making raids on various Bedouin tribes. This increased his prestige among the Arabs, and brought in booty, but otherwise they were of no political importance, and so we pass them by.

[1] *Moḥammed*, pp. 362–3. He gives *Muslim*, ii, 237, as the authority for the instructions to 'Alí.

In due course the time for the 'Umra, or Lesser Pilgrimage, came round. Some time before this, Muḥammad in a vision had seen himself making the circuit of the Ka'ba and performing all the usual ceremonies, so this pilgrimage is known as the 'Umratu'l-Qaḍá, or the fulfilled pilgrimage, as it was the fulfilment of the vision. In the spring of A.D. 629, therefore, Muḥammad with about two thousand followers approached Mecca.[1] The Quraish retired from the city and the Muslims, leaving their weapons outside, entered Mecca, which for seven years they had not seen. When Muḥammad came to the Ka'ba he said: 'May God be gracious to the man whom he shows to them (the Meccans) to-day in his strength.' He performed the usual ceremonies of the pagan pilgrimage, such as kissing the black stone, making the seven prescribed circuits of the Ka'ba, and the running between the mounts Ṣafá and Marwa. The animals brought for the purpose were sacrificed, and the ceremonies of the Lesser Pilgrimage were brought to an end. The honour paid to the city and to the ancient temple favourably influenced the Meccans; the friendships formed, through his marriage now with Maimúna—the fourth addition to his ḥarem during this year—advanced his cause, and when Muḥammad retired again to Madína he was much more

[1] See Muir, *The Life of Mahomet*, vol. iv, pp. 83-92.

powerful in every way than he had been at any previous period. One result of this pilgrimage, or of the marriage with Maimúna, was that her nephew Khalíd ibn Walíd and Amír ibn ʻÁṣ, both famous cavalry leaders, became Muslims.

THE SARIYA OF MUTA

The next event of importance was the Sariya-i-Múta. Muḥammad sent Ḥáritha bin ʻUmair with a letter to the Ghassánide ruler of Bostra, calling upon him to embrace Islám now. On arriving at Múta the Ghassánide chief of the place, Shuraḥbíl, said to be an official in the service of the emperor Heraclius, put Ḥáritha to death. When the news reached Muḥammad, he at once gave orders for the departure of a force of three thousand men. He placed Zaid bin Ḥáritha in command. In case he fell Jaʻfar bin Abi Ṭálib was to succeed, and, if necessary, ʻAbdu'lláh bin Rawáha. If all three fell the army was to choose its own commander. It is said that Muḥammad made this arrangement by the direct order of God or by inspiration.[1] The conquest of Khaibar and raids in the direction of the Syrian border[2] had no doubt caused some alarm to the tribes of that

[1] بوحی یا الهام *Mudáriju'n-Nabúwat*, p. 737.

[2] The Ghazwa-i-Bani Judzám and the Ghazwa-i-Bani Fezára show that the Syrians had just cause for anxiety. See Muir's *The Life of Mahomet*, vol. iv, pp. 10–13.

region, and so Shuraḥbíl had no difficulty in gathering together a large force. The Muslim leaders now realized that they had not to contend with a petty chief, but with some, at least, of the imperial forces. Some suggested a return to Mecca, but this was overruled by 'Abdu'lláh bin Abi Rawáha, who said: 'What have we marched for thus far.' Is it our numbers, or the help of the Lord in which we trust? Then forward!' So they proceeded to the attack with the result that they gained no victory. The historians try and make out that the Muslims won the day and then retired; but the reception of the returning army at Madína does not support this view. They were met with the cry: 'Ah ye runaways! Do you indeed flee before the enemy when fighting for the Lord.' They brought back no booty, a sign of victory absent on this occasion. The three commanders were slain, but Khalíd, a skilful commander, by ingenious and rapid movements, saved his forces and escaped destruction. When the defeated army reached Madína the sorrow was great. Muḥammad is said to have had, in some supernatural way, information of all that was going on during the time of the battle itself.[1] He felt acutely the loss of his cousin Ja'far and of Zaid, his old and trusted friend. The story of his grief, as told by the historians, is very touching.

[1] Muir, *The Life of Mahomet*, vol. iv, p. 101.

Both the Right Honourable Syed Amír 'Alí and Maulaví Cherágh 'Alí justify the expedition to Múta as one made to punish the murder of a messenger or envoy.[1] We possess no records of the Syrian view of the case, nor of the reason for the act, but it was known that the Muslims were gradually making raids and conquests in the direction of the Syrian border, and this man may very likely have been looked upon as a spy. In any case he was an enemy. Now, there had been many assassinations of men opposed to Muḥammad, either under the order or, at least, with the connivance of Muḥammad himself. Cherágh 'Alí defends all these on the ground that these men were fomenters of strife. They were Abú Afak, Ka'b bin Ashraf, Sufyán bin Khalíd, Abú Ráfi' and others.[2] If the murder of the Muslim messenger at Múta was wrong, all these others were wrong also, and this we hold to be the case; but to blame the Syrians for doing that for which they could, no doubt, have given some reason, and to exonerate Muḥammad for the assassination of men, who had a perfect right to be in opposition to him, and to strive for the defence of their homes and their

[1] *Critical Exposition of Jehád*, p. 139; *Life and Teaching of Moḥammed*, p. 191.

[2] *Critical Exposition of Jehád*, pp. 65, 66, 69, 71.

property, is scarcely the way to treat historical events with impartiality. Both were right or both were wrong.

THE CAPTURE OF MECCA

The impression caused by a disaster had to be speedily removed, and another expedition likely to result in success was the best available remedy. He no doubt saw that his attack on Syria was premature, and that before entering on conquests abroad, his position must first be made stronger in Arabia. Then came a revelation in this very short Súra, the Súratu'n-Naṣr (cx) :—

> When the help of God, and the victory[1] arrive, and thou seest men entering the religion of God by troops.
> Then utter the praise of the Lord and implore His pardon, for He loveth to turn in mercy.

Thus encouraged, he was able to proceed. Undoubtedly the unity of the political community, the consolidation of his followers as a religious corporation needed a centre other than Madína. The time had now come when, if Islám was to be the one politico-religious force in Arabia, which Muḥammad had from the first intended it to be, Mecca must become its centre.

He saw that the Meccans were now weary of strife, that many Quraish leaders were either

[1] Baiḍáwí says that the victory is that of Mecca, and that 'by troops' is meant the men of Mecca, of Ṭá'if, Yaman, Hawázin and all the Arab tribes.

dead or had joined him, that everywhere in the country his own power was extending, and that it would be now possible by a determined effort to capture Mecca and once for all break down the remaining opposition of the Quraish.

The thirteenth Súra is the last Meccan one, but the forty-first verse is interpolated and probably refers to this period:—

> See they not that we come to the land and diminish the borders thereof? God judges and there is none to reverse His judgement, and He is swift at reckoning up.—Suratu'r-Ra'd (xiii) 41.

Ibn 'Abbás[1] and other commentators refer this to the Meccans, who were so blind and obtuse that they did not realize that the Muslims were encroaching more and more on the territories of the pagan Arab tribes. Ḥusain, however, says it refers to the Jews, whose forts, lands and possessions had now come into the possession of the Muslims.

Some, apparently, were very reluctant to join in this expedition and are thus reproved:—

> What, will ye not fight against those (Meccans) who have broken their oaths and aimed to expel your Apostle, and attacked you first? Will ye dread them? God is more worthy of your fear, if ye are believers. So make war on them: by your hands will God chastise them and will put them to shame, and will give you victory over them.—Suratu't-Tauba (ix) 13–14.

[1] *Tafsir-i-Ḥusaini*, vol. i, p. 343.

Those who took an active part in the attack on Mecca and shared in the victory over it are highly praised, and their conduct is favourably contrasted with those who gave alms and fought for Islám after this event had shown the power of the Prophet :—

> Those amongst you who contributed before the victory and fought shall be differently treated from others amongst you: they are grander in rank than those who gave and fought afterwards.—Suratu'l-Hadid (lvii) 10.

Two years had passed since the treaty of Ḥudaibiya was made and, according to its terms, the peace between Madína and Mecca was to last for ten years. This difficulty was overcome. A Bedouin tribe attached to Muḥammad was attacked by another tribe in alliance with the Quraish. The Prophet seized the occasion, took up the quarrel, and with a large army of some ten thousand men advanced against Mecca. Abú Sufyán, the old and implacable enemy of the Prophet, saw that the time for opposition was past. He sought for an interview with Muḥammad, repeated the Muslim creed, and became henceforth a good Muslim. This led to the comparatively quiet submission of Mecca where Abú Sufyán, the hereditary leader of the Quraish, possessed great influence. As soon as Muḥammad entered the city he proceeded to the Ka'ba and saluted the black stone. He then ordered all the idols to be hewn down and, in order to show that he now exercised supreme authority, he appointed 'Uthmán bin Ṭalḥa and 'Abbás to the two hereditary offices connected with the temple.[1]

A crier then proclaimed in the streets this order: 'Whoever believeth in God and in the last day, let him not leave in his house any image whatever that he doth not break in pieces.[2]

Many of the Meccans mocked, and then a revelation came to show that by nature all men are equal, and that in the sight of God noble birth and pride of race or rank is of little worth as compared with the fear of the Lord. The Quraish are rebuked in :—

> O men, Verily we have created you of a male and a female; and we have divided you into peoples and tribes that ye might have knowledge one of another Truly, the most worthy of honour in the sight of God is he who feareth Him most.—Suratu'l-Hujurat (xlix) 14.

In reply to a question asking the Meccans what they thought of him, Muḥammad received the answer from some of them: 'We think well of thee, O noble brother and son of a noble brother. Verily thou hast obtained power over us.'

1 It is said that this transaction is referred to and justified in :—

'Verily, God enjoineth you to give back your trusts to their owners'.—Súratu'n-Nisá' (iv) 61.

2 Muir, *The Life of Mahomet*, vol. iv, p. 129.

Referring to the Súratu Yúsuf (xii) the Prophet quoted the words in the ninety-second verse, which were said by Joseph to his brethren:—

> No blame be on you this day. God will forgive you, for He is the most merciful of those who show mercy.—Suratu Yusuf (xii) 92.

With a few exceptions,[1] mostly of those who, it must be admitted, deserved their fate, a general amnesty extended to all the inhabitants of the city. The result was that the Prophet soon won the hearts of the people. There were no Munáfiqún in Mecca as there had been in Madína. It was a day of great triumph to Muḥammad, for now had the mercy of God come upon them. Eight years before he had left Mecca as a fugitive, a despised outcast. Since then the Quraish had been unwearying in their opposition, and now that was at an end. The sacred city was in his possession and his word was law. He had stood in the temple, sacred for many centuries to the worship of al-Lát and al-'Uzzá and a host of inferior deities, and with a word had banished idolatry from it for ever. He, by his own authority, had now appointed officers to it, and made it the centre of the new religion. No wonder that success so great caused Islám to spread most rapidly now. At last it seemed as

[1] About ten persons. See *The Historical Development of the Qur'án* (3rd ed.), pp. 196–7.

if the Arab people would be united as they had never been before; at last the patriotic feelings of the Prophet seemed near their realization, and Arabia united and free—a political and a religious whole—would more than resist the enemies who but a few years before had been encroaching on her territories, and threatening her very existence. 'The taking of Mecca was the outcome of a series of events which began on the day when Muḥammad was allowed to become the master of a community that lay between the Kuraish and their markets . . . The historians tell us little of the internal history of Mecca during the past eight years, whence the gradual shift of opinion in Muḥammad's favour can only be guessed. We are justified in supposing that much was effected by Muḥammad's campaigns against the Byzantines, which, though not immediately successful, made him the champion of a national idea.'[1]

THE GHAZWA OF HUNAIN

The capture of Mecca and the consolidation of the Muslim State caused some anxiety to some of the neighbouring Bedouin tribes, lest their ancient liberties should be endangered. It is related that they said: 'Muḥammad has vanquished the Quraish; after he has completed their

[1] Margoliouth, *Moḥammed*, pp. 388–9.

subjugation, he will probably turn against us: therefore it will be suitable that we attack him ere he prepares his army and marches towards us.'[1] About a fortnight after Mecca had fallen, the Baní Hawázin and the Baní Thaqíf, who inhabited Tá'if, assembled together under the command of Málik ibn 'Auf Naḍari. The Muslim army of 10,000 strong which had come to Mecca was reinforced by 2,000 more from the inhabitants of that city. The forces of the enemy are placed at about 4,000. They waited the approach of the Muslim army in ambush in the valley of Ḥunain. The Muslim being taken unawares met with a severe repulse and a panic set in. They fled in confusion, and it seemed as if the day was lost; but the Prophet bade his uncle 'Abbás cry out: 'O! men of Madína! O! men of the tree of fealty! O! men of the Súratu'l-Baqara!' The flight of some was arrested, and then Muḥammad, ascending a mound and taking some gravel in his hand, cast it towards the enemy, and said: 'Ruin seize them.' A body of devoted warriors rallied round him. The tide of battle turned and the enemy were, after a hard struggle, utterly routed. As usual, a revelation came in connexion with this battle, and the initial reverse is attributed to the vainglory the Muslims showed in their numbers. Thus:—

> Now hath God helped you on many battle-fields, and on the day of Hunain, when ye prided yourselves on

[1] *Rauḍatu'ṣ-Ṣafá*, part II, vol. ii, p. 617.

your numbers; but it availed you nothing, and the earth with all its breadth became too strait for you; then turned ye your backs in flight.—Suratu'l-Tauba (ix) 25.

In the next verse the final victory is attributed to supernatural aid:—

Then did God send down His spirit of repose[1] upon His apostle and upon the faithful, and He sent down the hosts which ye saw not, and He punished the infidels.

THE GHAZWA OF TA'IF

The town of Tá'if, the head-quarters of the Baní Thaqíf, situated about a thirty-six hours' journey from Mecca, was strongly fortified and provisioned for a whole year. It also possessed a plentiful supply of water. The siege was protracted for some weeks, but all efforts to capture the city failed. Muḥammad sought advice from his leading men. One said: 'A fox in its hole: remain long enough and you will catch it: leave it alone and it will not harm you.' The Prophet had a dream which showed him that it was no use prolonging the siege. He caused a proclamation to be made that all slaves in the city who joined him should be made free, but less than twenty came, and so he raised the siege. About ten months after the people of Tá'if submitted to him.

The cause of Islám was too well assured to suffer from the raising of the siege. It showed,

[1] For a critical note on this phrase, see *The Historical Development of the Qur'án* (3rd ed.), pp. 198–9.

however, what a few brave men could do, and had the men of Mecca been as stout of heart as the Baní Thaqíf of Tá'if, that city need never have fallen and the cause of Islám might have received, if not a fatal blow, at least a very severe check.

There was probably some disappointment at the failure to capture Tá'if and the property to be found in it; but the Prophet, who had with much forethought postponed the division of the rich booty captured at Ḥunain, was now in a position to reward his new allies. He gave large presents to the leading chiefs of Mecca and of the Bedouin tribes, who had become converts, at which his old followers and friends were somewhat annoyed and discontented. But later on a revelation came to justify his action, even in a small matter like this:—

> Some of them defame thee in regard to the alms, yet if a part be given them, they are content, but if no part be given them, behold, they are angry. . . .
>
> Would that they were satisfied with what God and His Apostle had given them and would say, 'God sufficeth us, God will vouchsafe to us of His favour, and so will His Apostle: verily unto God do we make our suit.'
>
> But alms are only to be given to the poor and needy and those who collect them, and to those whose hearts are reconciled (to Islam).[1]—Suratu't-Tauba (ix) 58-60.

[1] It is the unanimous opinion of the commentators that the words الْمُؤلفَة قُلوبهم 'whose hearts are reconciled', mean won over to Islám.

The alms were, in the case of the chiefs who received rich presents, very much of the nature of a tribe, and naturally the men of Madína objected to the procedure. The words 'those whose hearts are reconciled to Islám' are said by the commentators to be now abrogated, for Abú Bakr abolished the making of these gifts to converts, because God had now prospered Islám, and so such gifts were no longer needed.[1]

THE GHAZWA OF TABUK

A certain amount of discontent had arisen in Madína, owing to the defeat at Múta, the failure to capture Tá'if and the preference shown to recent Meccan and Bedouin converts in the distribution of the spoils of Ḥunain. A fresh expedition with the prospect of gain was evidently the best way to allay such unrest and to divert the minds of the men of Madína from their real or supposed wrongs. Towards the end of the ninth year of the Hijra, rumours reached Madína that the emperor Heraclius was collecting a large army on the Syrian frontier and intended to advance against Madína. As the sequel shows the rumour was false.[2] Probably it was believed at the time, and so Muḥammad availed himself

[1] See for authorities for this statement *The Historical Development of the Qur'án*, pp. 200–1.

[2] *Rauḍatu's-Ṣafá*, part II, vol. ii, p. 655.

of the cpportunity to make this Ghazwa and to exhibit to the Greeks and the Bedouins his growing power. He usually concealed the object of such expeditions, but as the distance to Tabúk, a place midway between Madína and Damascus, was great, and the difficulties of the march extreme and many, and provisions on the way were scarce, in this case he made known his intention. So great were the anticipated difficulties that the expedition is known by the name of 'The Ghazwa of distress'.[1] Levies were called in from various tribes, and good Muslims gave supplies. Abú Bakr gave his whole property and 'Umar devoted one-half of his to the cause. Their example was followed by many others,[2] and Muḥammad found himself at the head of a comparatively well-equipped army said to consist of 30,000 warriors. Still great and numerous as the gifts had been, all who wished to go could not be provided for. Those whose services could not be utilized in the expedition to Tabúk wept bitterly, and were ever after called al-Baká'ún 'The weepers'. They are told that no blame attaches to those:—

> To whom when they came to thee thou didst say, 'I find not wherewith to mount you', and they turned

[1] غزوة العسرة

[2] A full account of the gifts will be found in the *Rauḍatu's-Ṣafá*, (part II, vol. ii, pp. 652-3), and in the *Mudáriju'n-Nabúwat*, pp. 704-5.

away their eyes shedding floods of tears for grief, because they found no means to contribute.—Suratu't-Tauba (ix) 93.

But amongst those who went some were half-hearted, one said to his friends: 'This man wants to conquer the forts and districts of the country of Syria, which is not likely to happen.' Then one who was present rebuked the speaker, and said that he hoped some verse would be revealed concerning such wicked conversation. Meanwhile, Muḥammad had been supernaturally informed of this murmuring. On knowing this, the hypocrites were afraid and said that they had spoken only in fun. Then came the revelation:—

> The hypocrites are afraid lest a Sura should be sent down concerning them to tell plainly what is in their hearts. Say: scoff ye, but God will bring to light that which ye are afraid of.
>
> And if thou question them, they will surely say, 'We were only discoursing and jesting.' Say, what! do ye scoff at God,[1] and His signs, and His Apostle.
>
> Make no excuse: from faith ye have passed to infidelity. If we forgive some of you, we will punish others; for that they have been evil doers.—Suratu't-Tauba (ix) 65–7.

In due course the army after much difficulty and suffering arrived at Tabúk and found no

[1] This apparently claims divine approval of the warlike expedition to Tabúk, for, according to Baiḍáwí, it was that which was the cause of the jesting.

enemy there.[1] It stayed there, according to some accounts, two months; according to others twenty days. As the Ghazwa was quite profitless, it was thought desirable to make a demonstration against Christians and Jews. John, the Christian Prince of Ailah, made a treaty with the Prophet and agreed to pay an annual tribute. The most interesting embassy to the Prophet was that of the Christians of Najrán headed by their Bishop, Abú Háritha. They refused to accept Islám or to agree to Muḥammad's proposal, 'Come let us curse each other and lay the curse of Alláh on those that lie.' Finally, they agreed to pay the poll-tax which all non-Muslims had to give.[2]

This event is referred to in the following verses of the Qur'án:—

> Verily, Jesus is as Adam in the sight of God. He created him of dust; He then said to him, 'Be, and he was'.
>
> The truth is from thy Lord. Be not thou, therefore, of those who doubt.
>
> As for those who dispute with thee about Him,[3] after the knowledge hath come to thee, say, 'Come, let us

1 The *Raudatu's-Ṣafá* (part II, vol. ii, pp. 661–4) gives a vivid description of extraordinary miracles which took place during the march. These may be dismissed as fabulous, but the record of them shows the importance attached to this Ghazwa by the early historians. Maulaví Cherágh 'Alí calls such accounts 'the inventions of a playful fantasy'.

2 *Raudatu's-Ṣafá*, part II, vol. ii, p. 687; *Baiḍáwí*, vol. i, p. 109.

3 i.e. after knowing Jesus is a prophet and a servant (not divine) see *Tafsír-i-Ḥusainí*, vol. i, p. 70.

از دانستن عیسی که رسول و بنده است

> summon our sons and your sons, our wives and your wives, and ourselves and yourselves. Then will we invoke and lay the curse of God on those who lie.'—Suratu Ali 'Imran (iii) 52–4.[1]

At the same time an expedition[2] under Khálid bin Walíd was made to Dúmatu'l-Jandal, in consequence of which the Christian Prince Ukaidir accepted Islám. Khálid promised him his life if he did so, but he had to deliver up his fortresses, his arms and horses and unoccupied lands.[3] As this prince had not taken up arms, nor in any way interfered with the Muslims, it was a clear case of conversion by the sword. Several Jewish tribes also now submitted to the Prophet's rule and became dhimmís. Although Muḥammad was thus able to show that the Ghazwa of Tabúk was not altogether fruitless, and on his return heard the good news of the submission of the Baní Thaqíf,[3] yet there were indications that to some of the people of Madína the actions of the Prophet were unpopular, so now some of the disaffected—the Munáfiqún—at Madína, who had not followed the Prophet in this expedition, on his return home, were severely rebuked. Special revelations, which commentators agree in referring to the war of Tabúk,[4] came to reprove them,

[1] The fifty-fourth verse is called the Áyatu'l-Mubáhalat, or the 'verse of imprecation'.

[2] *Mudáriju'n-Nabúwat*, p. 812.

[3] On the terms of the submission, see Margoliouth, *Moḥammed*, p. 429.

[4] *Khatáṣatu't-Tafásir*, vol. i, p. 256.

and the Arabs of the desert also, and to warn others:—

O Believers! what possessed you, that when it was said to you, 'March forth on the way of God', ye sank heavily earthwards? What! prefer ye the life of this world to the next?

Unless ye march forth, with a grievous chastisement will He chastise you, and he will place another people in your stead, and ye shall in no way harm Him: for over everything God is potent.[1]

March ye forth the light and heavy armed, and contend with your substance and your persons on the way of God. This, if ye know it, will be better for you.

'Had there been a near advantage and a short journey, they would certainly have followed thee, but the way seemed long to them, yet will they swear by God: 'Had we been able, we had surely gone forth with you;' they are self-destroyers. And God knoweth that they are surely liars.

God forgive thee! Why didst thou give them leave to stay behind, ere they who made true excuses had become known to thee, and thou hadst known the liars?

They only will ask thy leave who believe not in God and in the last day, and whose hearts are full of doubts and who are tossed up and down in their doubtings.

1 This verse is said to be abrogated by the ninety-second verse which makes some exceptions:—

It shall be no crime in the weak and in the sick and in those who find not the means of contributing to stay at home, provided they are sincere with God and His apostle.—Súratu't-Tauba (ix) 92.

Moreover, had they been desirous to take the field, they would have got ready for that purpose the munitions of war. But God was averse to their marching forth and made them laggards.

Had they taken the field with you, they would only have added a burden to you and have hurried about among you, stirring you up to sedition.—Suratu't-Tauba (ix) 38-9; 41-3; 45-7.

They who were left at home were delighted to stay behind God's Apostle, and were averse from contending with their riches and their persons for the cause of God and said, 'March not out in the heat'. Say, 'A fiercer heat will be the fire of hell.' Would that they understood this.—Suratu't-Tauba (ix) 82.

When a Sura was sent down with 'Believe in God and go forth to war with the Apostle', those of them who are possessed of riches demanded exemption and said, 'Allow us to be with those who sit at home'.—Suratu't-Tauba (ix) 87.

This was the last time Muḥammad led in person an expedition. It was followed by a few Sariyas of small importance. The Prophet then made the pilgrimage to Mecca and thus established the Hajj as one of the cardinal duties of Islám.[1]

THE SARIYA OF USAMA

After this was concluded, he returned to Madína and determined to organize an expedition against the Byzantines, known as the Sariya of Usáma

[1] For an account of this event, see Muir, *The Life of Mahomet*, vol. iv, pp. 230-43; Sell's *Historical Development of the Qur'án* (3rd ed.), pp. 236-45; Margoliouth's *Moḥammed*, pp. 444-6 and any Muslim Life of the Prophet.

bin Zaid. The defeat at Múta was still remembered, and it was desirable that some action should be taken to cause it to be forgotten by a more successful Sariya. It was placed under the command of Usáma, the son of Zaid who had been slain at Múta. The Prophet addressed him thus: 'March in the direction of Múta where thy father was slain. Attack the enemies, set fire to their habitations and goods. Make haste to surprise the people before the news reaches them.'[1]

But Muḥammad was now seized with his last illness and the expedition never set forth. The wars of the Prophet were now ended.

The verdict on these G͟hazwas and Sariyas naturally depends on the standpoint from which it is given. If we look upon Muḥammad in the dry light of history as an Arab chief, seeking to consolidate the various Arab tribes into a nation, strong to resist the various outside forces which were pressing upon them, by reason of their greater political unity and by an improved social condition, we must admit that there was some justification for some, at least, of these wars, sieges and raids and that he successfully attained his object.

But it is claimed by all Muslims that Muḥammad was more than a successful Arab Shaik͟h;

[1] *Rauḍatu's-Ṣafá*, part II, vol. ii, p. 702.

he was, in their opinion, an accredited Prophet of God, sent to found a new religion, or, as they would put it, to revive and purify the religion of Abraham. For this purpose, it is said, that he received through the Angel Gabriel direct commands from God,[1] and when no such direct orders came was still supernaturally guided by a subjective inspiration.[2] So, then, it is from this standpoint that the whole subject must be viewed. Again the actions of the Prophet, as well as his words, other than when giving forth the verses of the Qur'án, form the Sunnat, or divine rule of faith and practice for all Muslims for all time. This differentiates all these wars, sieges and raids from anything like them in Jewish or in Christian history, which form no rule of faith or practice for Christians. The spirit of Christianity does not accept the wars of Israel as a guide, nor does it look upon cruelties practised by nominal Christian rulers as a Sunnat—a divine rule of faith and practice, forming a basis of canon or of civil law. The *tu quoque* argument has no logical force here. We have shown again and again that the Qur'án, believed to be the very words of God, accepts full responsibility for what was done. Whilst admitting that many traditions may not have great historical value, yet those

1 That is by the waḥi (وحی) form of inspiration.

2 Ilhám (الهام).

which refer to the intervention of Gabriel show, at least, that the narration of them expressed the common belief that he was an active agent, as God's messenger to the Prophet.

Muḥammad thus stands out unique, amongst the founders of those religions which prevail at the present time among large populations, as the one who established his position by force of arms; and by claiming divine authority for so doing, has made such a procedure a sacred law, when circumstances allow of it, for all lands and all time.